POCKET EDITION

JACKSON'S HALLMARKS

ENGLISH, SCOTTISH, IRISH
SILVER & GOLD MARKS
FROM 1300 TO THE PRESENT DAY

edited by Ian Pickford

ANTIQUE COLLECTORS' CLUB

© Antique Collectors' Club 1991
World copyright reserved
First published in hardback 1991
Reprinted 1991, 1992
First published in paperback 1992
Reprinted 1993, 1994

Hardback ISBN 1 85149 128 7

Paperback ISBN 1 85149 169 4

Published for the Antique Collectors' Club
by the Antique Collectors' Club Ltd.

British Library Cataloguing in Publication Data:
A catalogue record for this book is available from the British Library

Printed in England by the Antique Collectors' Club Ltd.
5 Church Street, Woodbridge, Suffolk IP12 1DS

Antique Collectors' Club

The Antique Collectors' Club was formed in 1966 and now has a five figure membership spread throughout the world. It publishes the only independently run monthly antiques magazine *Antique Collecting* which caters for those collectors who are interested in widening their knowledge of antiques, both by greater awareness of quality and by discussion of the factors which influence the price that is likely to be asked. The Antique Collectors' Club pioneered the provision of information on prices for collectors and the magazine still leads in the provision of detailed articles on a variety of subjects.

It was in response to the enormous demand for information on ''what to pay'' that the price guide series was introduced in 1968 with the first edition of *The Price Guide to Antique Furniture* (completely revised 1978 and 1989), a book which broke new ground by illustrating the more common types of antique furniture, the sort that collectors could buy in shops and at auctions rather than the rare museum pieces which had previously been used (and still to a large extent are used) to make up the limited amount of illustrations in books published by commercial publishers. Many other price guides have followed, all copiously illustrated, and greatly appreciated by collectors for the valuable information they contain, quite apart from prices. The Antique Collectors' Club also publishes other books on antiques, including horology and art reference works, and a full book list is available.

Club membership, which is open to all collectors, costs £19.50 per annum. Members receive free of charge *Antique Collecting,* the Club's magazine (published ten times a year), which contains well-illustrated articles dealing with the practical aspects of collecting not normally dealt with by magazines. Prices, features of value, investment potential, fakes and forgeries are all given prominence in the magazine.

Among other facilities available to members are private buying and selling facilities, the longest list of ''For Sales'' of any antiques magazine, an annual ceramics conference and the opportunity to meet other collectors at their local antique collectors' clubs. There are over eighty in Britain and more than a dozen overseas. Members may also buy the Club's publications at special pre-publication prices.

As its motto implies, the Club is an amateur organisation designed to help collectors get the most out of their hobby: it is informal and friendly and gives enormous enjoyment to all concerned.

For Collectors — By Collectors — About Collecting

The Antique Collectors' Club, 5 Church Street, Woodbridge, Suffolk

Contents

Acknowledgements

My thanks must go to Henry Fothringham, Michael McAleer, the late Kurt Ticher, Timothy Kent, G.N. Barrett, Canon Maurice Ridgway, Martin Gubbins and Dr. Margaret Gill.

I am indebted to the Wardens of the Worshipful Company of Goldsmiths for their permission to quote from their records; also to Miss Susan Hare, Past Librarian of the Worshipful Company of Goldsmiths, and to David Beasley, Librarian.

Additional thanks should go to David W. Evans, Deputy Warden, Dr. Frank William Bennett, past Deputy Warden and Mr. David Barnes Dalladay, past Assistant Deputy Warden of the Worshipful Company of Goldsmiths for their assistance in the updating of the London hallmarks.

Particular thanks must go to Mr. Arthur Grimwade, Mr. John Culme, Mr. Anthony Dove, Mr. Brand Inglis, Mr. John Cooper, the Assay Master of Sheffield; Mr. David Johnson, and Molly Pearce, Keeper of Applied Arts, Weston Park Museum, Sheffield, for their advice on Sheffield; Mr. Jeremy Pearson and Mr. Richard Rendel for their help in the West Country (Exeter).

In addition Captain R. Le Bas of the Dublin Assay Office, Mr. Brian Beet, Ann Bennett, the Guardians of Birmingham Assay Office, the Birmingham University Field Archaeology Unit, Mr. Geoffrey Corbett, Mr. H.L. Douch, Mr. Robin Emmerson, Mr. John Forbes, Mrs. Phillipa Glanville, Mr. Richard Gray, the Laing Art Gallery, the Manchester City Art Galleries, Catherine Ross of the Laing Art Gallery, members of the NADFAS Church Recorders, the late Charles Oman, Mr. Michael Newman, The Shrewsbury Museum, Mr. Eric Smith, Mr. Peter Waldron, Mr. Donald Wilson and Mr. Richard Vander all receive acknowledgement for help given.

Ian Pickford, 1991

Preface

The object in producing this pocket edition of *Jackson's* has been to provide the information most likely to be needed when travelling, in a form that is both quick and easy to use.

Complete cycles of silver marks are given for all the important assay offices, with footnotes where necessary showing variations for gold, platinum, Britannia standard, import marks, etc.

For the smaller centres a selection of marks has been chosen in each case to give the most important variations likely to be found.

After the cycles of marks of each assay office a selection of makers' marks is given. These marks include not only the famous and important or interesting makers' names, but also the most prolific manufacturers and retailers, thus providing a good chance of finding a particular maker's mark in this section.

Since the vast majority of pieces to be found are from the 18th century and later, the makers' marks have, with only a few exceptions, been chosen from the post-1697 period.

In addition to the mark/marks of a maker, the period in which he/she was working has also been given in general terms, e.g. early 18th century or second quarter 19th century ('early 18th C' or '2nd ¼ 19th C'), as exact years of commencement, or more often cessation of work have not always been known.

The comments, where given, after a particular maker are to indicate such things as type of work produced (e.g. spoonmaker), how important that maker may be, whether prolific or rare, possible confusion with other makers, and any particular points to look for, e.g. a connection with an important designer.

Should any more detailed explanation, further variation of hallmarks, or makers' marks not given, be required, then reference to the main volume of *Jackson's* will, of course, be necessary.

Ian Pickford
1991

Understanding Hallmarks

Probably the easiest way to understand the hallmarking system in Britain is to examine its development in London and then observe how it was applied elsewhere.

The system is an ancient one. The first known statute governing standards was in 1238, although there were certainly controls on the workers in precious metals prior to this.

At this stage (in the 13th century) there were no official marks as such. Makers would, however, sometimes engrave their name and perhaps place of working on the piece. The Dolgelly chalice is a good example. Made in about 1250 it is engraved underneath 'NICOL'VS ME FECIT DE HER FORDIE', i.e. 'Nicholas of Hereford made me'.

The end of the 13th century saw the introduction of a marking system. Current research indicates that the reasons for it were to assist customs officials in preventing the export of silver from England (see *Jackson's,* pp.19-21).

The mark introduced in 1300 was a leopard's head. This mark was to be struck on silver of the standard of coinage or better, and gold of the touch of Paris (19.2 carats) or better, throughout the realm.

It is interesting to notice that both gold and silver were to receive the same mark and that it was to be used throughout the country, not just in London.

Using the standard of coinage (sterling, i.e. 92.5% silver content) for silver was important, since it allowed the ready interchange of goldsmiths' work (silver vessels, etc.) into coins and vice versa as the economic situation, either personal or national, required.

All known examples of leopards' head marks up to 1478 are in circular punches, the very earliest (c.1300-60) being plain circular (Figure 1) and those after about 1360 in a beaded, circular punch (Figure 2).

Figure 1

To help prevent the forgery of leopards' head marks, which were being struck on substandard wares by unscrupulous goldsmiths, a statute was passed in 1363. By this statute every master goldsmith was to have a mark of his own by which his work could be recognised. These early makers' marks were all symbols, for it was only with the spread of literacy that initials started to appear in the late 15th to early 16th century. Clearly then two marks were struck on a piece of silver or gold from 1363 onwards (see Figure 2).

Figure 2

For about the next century the system would appear to have worked well as it was not until 1478 that a further mark was added. This is what is referred to today as the date letter, which was introduced as the result of unscrupulous touch wardens (the men responsible for testing and marking silver and gold), in the second half of the 15th century, striking the leopard's head, for a financial consideration, on work which they knew to be below standard. This was easy for them to do at this time since the testing and marking were carried out in the goldsmiths' own shops. Apart from defrauding the customers there was the more serious long term effect (as happened also in the early 14th century), of these substandard wares being accepted from their marks as standard by the Mint and converted directly into coin. Ultimately this would lead to a loss of confidence in the currency and the dire national economic problems that would follow.

To stop this happening, important changes took place in 1478. First, the touch wardens were required to work in an office in the Goldsmiths' Hall. All goldsmiths then had to take their work to the Hall to have it marked (hence Hall Marks). Secondly, the leopard's head was given a crown and thirdly, a new mark — the date letter — was introduced (see Figure 3).

Figure 3

Originally this third mark was not to indicate the year in which the piece was tested, as it is today, but was the Assay Master's mark by which he could be identified should a properly marked piece be found to be below standard.

The Assay Master was sworn in annually in May. Since

the alphabetical letter by which he was identified moved on to the next letter, regardless of whether the same man was appointed, it is easy to see how these letters were later regarded as date letters.

The three marks of leopard's head, maker's mark and date letter remained the only marks in London from 1478 until 1544, when a fourth, the lion passant, was added to the system (Figure 4).

Figure 4   🄶 🦁 👑 🄸🄲

This, probably the most famous of all English marks, often referred to as the 'Sterling Lion', was added, not as a protection against fraud, but to show the Royal control that the Assay Office came under for a short period and which was retained thereafter.

What may be regarded as the Established System of marking sterling standard silver, was thus in operation from 1544 onwards. There was no further change to the system until the end of the 17th century. This change, the introduction of the Britannia standard in 1697, was radical, and resulted from the need to protect the coinage from being melted down to produce objects. The standard for silver was raised from 92.5% to 95.84% minimum silver content, whilst the silver coinage was retained at 92.5%, which meant that silver from coins could not be used for goldsmiths' work without refining, thus protecting it.

To demonstrate that this new standard was in force all the marks were changed (see Figure 5). The figure of Britannia replaced the sterling lion (hence Britannia standard) the lion's head erased replaced the crowned leopard's head. A new cycle of date letters was started just over a year earlier

Figure 5

than would normally have been the case and new makers' marks were registered, now the first two letters of the goldsmith's surname rather than his initials. (Note: Gold was not affected by this change and continued to be marked with the crowned leopard's head and lion passant guardant.)

In 1720 sterling was reintroduced as an alternative to the Britannia standard. Although the two standards have been in force from 1720 to the present day, little Britannia standard will be found between about 1735 and the end of the 19th century.

The year 1784 saw the introduction of a new but temporary mark, which was the duty mark, and was struck on silver to show that duty to pay for the American War of Independence had been paid. The mark chosen was the monarch's head and this will be found with successive heads struck on pieces up to 1890 (see Figure 6). Thus from 1784

Figure 6

to 1890 five marks will be found on a piece of London silver; this then reverts to four marks from 1890 to the present day.

There have been no really important changes to the marking of silver since 1890. Jubilee marks will be found in 1934-5 (Figure 7) and in 1977 (Figure 9). A coronation mark will be found in 1952-3 (Figure 8). These are, however, voluntary additional marks and not true hallmarks.

Figure 7   *Figure 8*   *Figure 9*

Distinct gold marking develops from the introduction of 18 carat gold in 1798. From 1300 up to this date it should be remembered that gold was marked in the same way as sterling standard silver (leaving aside the 1697-1720 period).

The 1973 Hallmarking Act which came into effect in 1975 brought about a number of changes. The most important of these was the introduction of platinum into the system. It has been given the distinct mark of an orb and cross within a pentagon (Figure 10).

By this same Act all Assay Offices now use the same date letter which represents a calendar year. The use of the lion's

Figure 10

head erased was also dropped from Britannia standard marking.

ENGLISH PROVINCIAL MARKS

Provincial marking in England may be divided into three periods:
(1) Prior to 1697
(2) 1697-1701-2
(3) 1701-2 to the present day

1. Prior to 1697
Many centres used marks. These range from the use of makers' marks only (often struck more than once on a piece), in some of the smaller centres, to proper cycles of marks, including the use of date letters found in major centres such as York.

2. 1697-1701-2
The Act introducing Britannia standard in 1697 unfortunately omitted any provision for marking in the provinces. It was therefore technically illegal for any of these centres to mark silver. The provinces appear to have ignored this, choosing rather to alter the character of the marks they were then using to make them less easily recognisable. (This causes great problems in identifying these marks today.)

3. 1701-2 to the present day
After the bungled Act of Parliament which had technically excluded the provinces from marking in 1697, a further Act was passed by which those centres which had a mint operating could also have an Assay Office. By this act from 1701 onwards Exeter, Bristol, Norwich, Chester, and York could all mark silver.

Unfortunately, this second act was a further bungle since it included Bristol and Norwich, neither of which could justify at this time the need for an Assay Office, and excluded Newcastle, which was then one of the most important provincial centres. A further Act was then passed specifically for Newcastle which was, as a result, able to mark from 1702 onwards. From that date all the minor centres were required to send items for marking to the official Assay Office in their area.

The marks required for the major centres were effectively the same as those used in London with the addition of a town mark. The actual shapes of punches, styles of letters, and cycles differ from those in London but the general character is the same.

In time all provincial centres stopped using the leopard's head; the last was in 1883.

SCOTLAND

Edinburgh
By an enactment of 1457 gold and silver of the required standard (20 carats for gold and 91.66% minimum silver content for silver) were to be marked with the deacon's mark and the maker's mark.

The Deacon was the chief office bearer of the craft within the town; he would normally be a working goldsmith and as such would use his 'maker's mark' as his Deacon's mark, when in office. Thus a marked piece of this early date (of which none is known) would have been marked with what would have the appearance of two makers' marks.

In 1485 the town mark was added to the above and from that date until 1681 three marks were struck on a piece (see Figure 11).

Figure 11

Exact dating of Edinburgh pieces to a particular year during this period can only occasionally be achieved due to Deacons being appointed for a number of years over a span of years.

1681 saw two important changes: first the introduction of cycles of date letters which continue to the present day, and secondly the replacement of the Deacon's mark by the Assay Master's mark.

The Assay Master would be a working goldsmith and, as with the Deacons before him, would use his maker's mark for this purpose. Pieces therefore continued to be struck with what appear to be two makers' marks together with the town mark and now with the addition of a date letter (Figure 12).

Figure 12

The Act of 1696 which introduced Britannia Standard to England was, of course, before the Act of Union and therefore was not applied in Scotland. However, the Act by which Sterling standard was reintroduced in 1720 was after the Act of Union. Scots goldsmiths, as a result of this Act, had to raise their standard to sterling. This did not, however, lead to any changes to any marks in Scotland.

In 1759 the thistle mark replaced the Assay Master's mark (see Figure 13); it in turn was replaced by a lion rampant in 1975. Otherwise from the second half of the 18th century onwards duty marks and optional marks follow what has been given for London.

Figure 13

Scots Provincial

Scotland is particularly rich in the number of centres which marked silver. Since the marks were produced by the silversmiths themselves there are no hard and fast rules to follow. The vast majority of pieces to be found date from the late 18th and early 19th centuries. During this period it was quite usual for a maker to stamp his own mark twice on the piece, together with his own town mark. Town marks divide into two groups, those which are an abbreviation of the name of the town and those based on the heraldry of the town.

The above are, however, very broad generalisations, exceptions to which will easily be found.

(Note: Some Indian Colonial marks may easily be mistaken for Scottish Provincial.)

IRELAND

Dublin
In 1605 it was decreed by the Dublin City Council that silver of the correct standard (coin) was to be marked with a lion, a harp and a castle together with a maker's mark.

To date no silver has been found bearing these marks.

By a new Charter of 1637 silver and gold was to be marked with a crowned harp (the King's standard mark) and a maker's mark. A year later a date letter was added to the above and it is from 1638 on that examples survive of Dublin hallmarks.

Figure 14

The above use of three marks (Figure 14) continued until 1730-1 when, to show that duty had been paid, the Hibernia mark was added thus giving four marks (Figure 15).

Figure 15

In 1807 Hibernia was replaced as a duty mark by the monarch's head (similar to that already in use in England and Scotland); it was not dropped but continued to be stamped as the 'town mark' of Dublin, providing until 1890, when the monarch's head was dropped, five marks (Figure 16).

Figure 16

(Note: Britannia standard never applied in Ireland. Hibernia punches can easily be mistaken for Britannia.)

Irish Provincial
Cork and Limerick both used similar styles of marks. During the late 17th to early 18th century a castle/castle turret mark, often repeated twice, was used in both. (A ship mark if found was only used in Cork.) With the castle mark,

a maker's mark will also be found which is often struck twice.

From the early 18th century to the early 19th century the word 'Sterling' (in full) was adopted by both centres and used with makers' marks which, as earlier, were often repeated twice.

With the similarity of marks in these two centres, distinguishing one from the other is best done by reference to the makers' marks (see *Jackson's*, pp.710-26). The majority of pieces from these two centres are from Cork; other Irish Provincial silver is only rarely found.

(Note: The word 'Sterling' is stamped on vast quantities of North American silver.)

GOLD MARKS

Gold and silver were, when of the required standard, struck with the same marks as each other until 1798. (The exception to this being the period 1697 to June 1720 during the compulsory Britannia standard for silver.)

The introduction of 18 carat gold in 1798 saw, for the first time, truly distinctive gold marking; 22 carat continued to be struck with the same marks as sterling standard silver until 1844.

However, in 1816 the assay master's note book records "Impressions of the Sun to be used from and after 29 of May 1816 on the 22 carat standard". This rare mark was struck in addition to the sterling standard type marks, and continued in use until the introduction of the crown and twenty-two (separate) punches in 1844.* Because of the demand for cheaper gold watch cases in America, 1854 saw the addition of 15, 12 and 9 carat to the standards for gold. The marks for these lower standards are quite distinct from the established 22 and 18 carats.

The 15 and 12 carat standards were used for the last time in 1932 when 14 carat was introduced.

No changes in standard have occurred since 1932 and so from 1933 to the present day, we have the four standards of 22, 18, 14 and 9 carats.

* This applies to London only.

PLATINUM MARKS

The 1973 hallmarking act brought for the first time platinum within the hallmarking system. A standard of 950 parts per thousand was introduced. The mark chosen was an orb and cross within a pentagon (used by all four assay offices) and the first pieces were marked in London on 2nd January 1975.

IMPORT MARKS

Imported plate was required in 1842 to be submitted for assay and marking before being sold in England, Scotland or Ireland (an exception was made of pre-1800 plate). There was no provision, however, in this act for an import mark, the current marks of the assay office to which the piece had been submitted being stamped.

It was by the Act of 1867 that an extra mark of F in an oval punch was required to be struck on imported wares of the correct standard.

The whole system was radically reformed by "The Hallmarking of Foreign Plate Act, 1904". By this act quite distinct import marks were introduced, Phoebus (the Sun) being used as the mark for London* (a square punch for gold and an oval punch for silver). Numerical punches were introduced for the standards. The current date letter was also struck.

Problems arose over the use of the sun mark (due to existing trade marks) as a result of which it was changed by Order in Council (11th May 1906) to the sign of the constellation Leo. The first Leo marks were actually produced with Leo upside down. Apart from the alterations in gold standards in 1932 and the addition of platinum and change in the style of the numerical punches in 1975, the system of import marks has remained the same to the present day.

* London is taken here as the example.

CONVENTION HALLMARKS

The United Kingdom, together with Austria, Denmark, Finland, Ireland, Norway, Portugal, Sweden and Switzerland have ratified the International Hallmarking Convention (the United Kingdom in 1976). By this convention special marks are legally recognised as approved hallmarks by the United Kingdom. Imported pieces bearing these marks do not, therefore, have to be submitted for import marking.

The convention marks struck in London comprise the Leopard's Head, the Common Control Mark, The Fineness mark (numerals showing the standard in parts per thousand) and the Sponsor's (i.e. maker's) mark.

It is possible for imported wares to be submitted for convention hallmarks. In this case the appropriate import mark replaces the leopard's head.

CHAPTER I

London

Cycles of Hallmarks

THE LEOPARD'S HEAD MARK
DATE ANTERIOR TO 1478
(The ascribed dates are approximate)

DATE	MARK
1300	
1300-50	
1350	
1400	
1450	
1470	

CYCLE I

	LEOPARD'S HEAD CROWNED	DATE LETTER
EDW.IV 1478-79		
1479-80		B
1480-81		C
1481-82		D
1482-83		
RICH.III 1483-84		
1484-85		
HEN.VII 1485-86		
1486-87		
1487-88		
1488-89	"	L
1489-90	"	M
1490-91	"	N
1491-92	"	O
1492-93		
1493-94	"	Q
1494-95	"	R
1495-96		S
1496-97		T
1497-98		

CYCLE II

	LEOPARD'S HEAD CROWNED	DATE LETTER
1498-99		a
1499-1500	"	b
1500-1	"	c
1501-2	"	d
1502-3		
1503-4	"	f
1504-5	"	g
1505-6		
1506-7		i
1507-8	"	k
1508-9		l
HEN.VIII 1509-10		m
1510-11	"	n
1511-12	"	o
1512-13	"	p
1513-14		q
1514-15	"	r
1515-16		s
1516-17	"	t
1517-18	"	u

CYCLE III   CYCLE IV

	LEOPARD'S HEAD CROWNED	DATE LETTER			LEOPARD'S HEAD CROWNED	DATE LETTER	LION PASSANT FROM 1544
1518-19	◯	A		1538-39	◯	A	
1519-20	◯	B		1539-40	◯	B	
1520-21	◯	C		1540-41	"	C	
1521-22	"	D		1541-42	"	D	
1522-23	"	E		1542-43		E	
1523-24	"	F		1543-44	"	F	
1524-25	"	G		1544-45*	"	G	◯
1525-26	"	h		1545-46	◯	H	◯
1526-27				1546-47	"	I	"
1527-28	"	K		EDW.VI 1547-48	"	K	
1528-29	"	L		1548-49	"	L	◯
1529-30	"	M		1549-50	"	M	"
1530-31	"	N		1550-51 ┊	◯	N	◯
1531-32	◯	O		1551-52	"	O	◯
					"	O	
1532-33	"	P		1552-53	"	P	◯
1533-34	"	Q		MARY 1553-54	"	Q	"
1534-35	"	R		1554-55	"	R	"
1535-36	"	S		1555-56	"	S	"
1536-37	"	T		1556-57	"	T	"
1537-38	"	V		1557-58	"	V	◯

* Variation: ◯ G

┊ There is a variant of the lion passant in a shaped shield.

CYCLE V

	LEOPARD'S HEAD CROWNED	DATE LETTER	LION PASSANT
ELIZ.I 1558-60		a	
1559-60	"	b	"
1560 to 6 Jan.1561	"	c	"
7 Jan. 1561- May 1561	"	d	"
June 1561-62	"	d	
1562-63		e	"
1563-64	"	f	"
1564-65	"	g	"
1565-66	"	h	"
1566-67	"	i	"
1567-68	"	kk	"
1568-69	"	l	"
1569-70	"	m	"
1570-71	"	n	"
1571-72	"	o	"
1572-73	"	p	"
1573-74	"	q	
1574-75	"	r	"
1575-76	"	s	"
1576-77	"	t	"
1577-78	"	u	"

CYCLE VI

	LEOPARD'S HEAD CROWNED	DATE LETTER	LION PASSANT
1578-79		A	
1579-80	"	B	"
1580-81	"	C	"
1581-82	"	D	"
1582-83	"	E	"
1583-84	"	F	"
	"	G	"
1584-85	"	G	"
1585-86	"	H	"
1586-87	"	I	"
1587-88	"	K	"
1588-89	"	L	"
1589-90	"	M	"
1590-91	"	N	"
1591-92	"	O	"
1592-93		P	
1593-94	"	Q	"
1594-95	"	R	
1595-96	"	S	"
1596-97	"	T	"
1597-98	"	V	"

CYCLE VII

	LEOPARD'S HEAD CROWNED	DATE LETTER	LION PASSANT
1598-99	🛡	A	🦁
1599-1600	"	B	🦁
1600-1	"	C	"
1601-2	"	D	🦁
1602-3	"	E	"
JAS.I 1603-4	"	F	"
1604-5	"	G	🦁
1605-6	"	h	"
1606-7	"	I	🦁
1607-8	"	K	"
1608-9	"	L	"
1609-10	"	M	"
1610-11	"	n	🦁
1611-12	"	O	"
1612-13	"	P	"
1613-14	"	Q	"
1614-15	"	R	"
1615-16	"	S	"
1616-17	"	T	"
1617-18	"	V	"

CYCLE VIII

	LEOPARD'S HEAD CROWNED	DATE LETTER	LION PASSANT
1618-19	🛡	a	🦁
1619-20	"	b b	"
1620-21	"	c	"
1621-22	"	d	"
1622-23	"	e	"
1623-24	"	f	"
1624-25	"	g	"
CHAS.I 1625-26	"	h	"
1626-27	"	i	"
1627-28	"	k k	"
1628-29	"	l	"
1629-30	"	m	"
1630-31	"	n	"
1631-32	"	o	"
1632-33	"	p	"
1633-34	"	q	"
1634-35	"	r	"
1635-36	"	s	"
1636-37	"	t	"
1637-38	"	v	"

CYCLE IX

	LEOPARD'S HEAD CROWNED	DATE LETTER	LION PASSANT
1638-39	🛡	A B	🦁
1639-40	"	B	"
1640-41	"	C	"
1641-42	"	D	"
1642-43	"	E	"
1643-44	"	ff	"
1644-45	"	G	"
1645-46	"	H	"
1646-47	"	I	"
1647-48	🛡	K	🦁
1648-49	"	L	"
COMWTH. 1649-50	"	M	"
1650-51	"	N	"
1651-52	"	O	"
1652-53	"	P	"
1653-54	"	Q	"
1654-55	"	R	"
1655-56	"	S	"
1656-57	"	T	"
1657-58	"	V	"

CYCLE X

	LEOPARD'S HEAD CROWNED	DATE LETTER	LION PASSANT
1658-59	🛡	A	🦁
1659 Up to 12 July 1660	"	B	"
CHAS.II From 13 July 1660 to 27 June 1661	"	C	"
From 28 June 1661-62	"	D	"
1662-63	"	E	🦁
1663-64	"	F	"
1664-65	"	G	"
1665-66	"	H	"
1666-67	"	I	"
1667-68	"	K	"
1668-69	🛡	L	🦁
1669-70	"	M	"
1670-71	"	N	"
1671-72	"	O	"
1672-73	"	P	"
1673-74	"	Q	"
1674-75	"	R	"
1675-76	"	S	"
1676-77	"	T	"
1677-78	"	V	"

CYCLE XI*

	LEOPARD'S HEAD CROWNED	DATE LETTER	LION PASSANT
1678-79		**a**	
1679-80	"	**b**	
1680-81		**c**	
1681-82	"	**d**	"
1682-83	"	**e**	"
1683-84	"	**f**	"
1684-85	"	**g**	"
JAS.II 1685-86	"	**h**	"
1686-87	"	**i**	"
1687-88	"	**k**	"
1688-89	"	**l**	"
WM.& MY. 1689-90		**m**	
1690-91	"	**n**	"
1691-92	"	**o**	"
1692-93	"	**p**	"
1693-94	"	**q**	"
1694-95	"	**r**	"
WM.III 1695-96	"	**s**	"
20 May 1696 to 27 March 1697	"	**t**	"

* Cycles XI-XXVI
Marks reproduced courtesy of the Worshipful Company of Goldsmiths
╪ (Only Britannia standard in force)

CYCLE XII

SILVER ╪			
	BRITANNIA	DATE LETTER	LION'S HEAD ERASED
27 March to 28 May 1697		**A**	
1697-98	"	**B**	"
1698-99	"	**C**	"
1699-1700	"	**D**	"
1700-1	"	**E**	"
1701-2	"	**FF**	"
ANNE 1702-3	"	**G**	"
1703-4	"	**H**	"
1704-5	"	**I**	"
1705-6	"	**K**	"
1706-7	"	**L**	"
1707-8	"	**M**	"
1708-9	"	**N**	"
1709-10	"	**O**	"
1710-11	"	**P**	"
1711-12	"	**Q**	"
1712-13	"	**R**	"
1713-14	"	**S**	"
GEO.I 1714-15	"	**T**	"
1715-16	"	**U**	"

GOLD (22ct.)			
	LEOPARD'S HEAD CROWNED	DATE LETTER	LION PASSANT
Date as Above		As Above	

CYCLE XIII

BRITANNIA STANDARD			
	BRITANNIA	DATE LETTER	LION'S HEAD ERASED
1716-17	🛡	A	🦁
1717-18	"	B	"
1718-19	"	C	"
1719-20	"	D	"
1720-21	"	E	"
1721-22	"	F	"
1722-23	"	G	"
1723-24	"	H	"
1724-25	"	I	"
1725-26	"	K	"
1726-27	"	L	"
GEO.II 1727-28	"	M	"
1728-29	"	N	"
1729-30	"	O	"
1730-31	"	P	"
1731-32	"	Q	"
1732-33	"	R	"
1733-34	"	S	"
1734-35	"	T	"
1735-36	"	V	"

GOLD			
	LEOPARD'S HEAD CROWNED	DATE LETTER	LION PASSANT
1716-17	👑	A	🦁
1717-18	"	B	"
1718-19	"	C	"
1719-20	"	D	"

STERLING STANDARD SILVER & GOLD (22ct)
(Until 1720, only Britannia Standard in force)

	LEOPARD'S HEAD CROWNED	DATE LETTER	LION PASSANT
1720-21	🛡	E	🦁
	👑	"	"
1721-22	"	F	🦁
1722-23	"	G	"
1723-24	"	H	"
1724-25	👑	I	🦁
1725-26	"	K	"
1726-27	👑	L	🦁
GEO.II 1727-28	"	M	"
1728-29	"	N	"
1729-30	👑	O	🦁
1730-31	"	P	"
1731-32	"	Q	"
1732-33	"	R	"
1733-34	"	S	"
1734-35	"	T	"
1735-36	"	V	"

CYCLE XIV

STERLING STANDARD SILVER & GOLD (22ct)			
	LEOPARD'S HEAD CROWNED	DATE LETTER	LION PASSANT
1736-37	🛡	a	🦁
1737-38	"	b	"
1738-39*	"	c	"
1739-40	"	d	"
	🦁	d	🦁
1740-41	"	e	"
1741-42	"	f	"
1742-43	"	g	"
1743-44	"	h	"
1744-45	"	i	"
1745-46	"	k	"
1746-47	"	l	"
1747-48	"	m	"
1748-49	"	n	"
1749-50	"	o	"
1750-51	"	p	"
1751-52*	"	q	"
1752-53	"	r	"
1753-54	"	ſ	"
1754-55	"	t	"
1755-56	"	u	"

BRITANNIA STANDARD SILVER			
	BRITANNIA	DATE LETTER	LION'S HEAD ERASED
Date as Above	🛡	As Above	🦁

CYCLE XV

STERLING STANDARD SILVER & GOLD (22ct)			
	LEOPARD'S HEAD CROWNED	DATE LETTER	LION PASSANT
1756-57	🛡	A	🦁
1757-58	"	B	"
1758-59*	"	C	"
1759-60*	"	D	"
GEO.III 1760-61	"	E	"
1761-62	"	F	"
1762-63	"	G	"
1763-64	"	H	"
1764-65	"	I	"
1765-66	"	K	"
1766-67	"	L	"
1767-68	"	M	"
1768-69	"	N	"
1769-70	"	O	"
1770-71	"	P	"
1771-72	"	Q	"
1772-73	"	R	"
1773-74	"	S	"
1774-75	"	T	"
1775-76	"	U	"

BRITANNIA STANDARD SILVER			
	BRITANNIA	DATE LETTER	LION'S HEAD ERASED
Date as Above	🛡	As Above	🦁

CYCLE XVI

STERLING STANDARD SILVER & GOLD (22ct)			
	LEOPARD'S HEAD CROWNED	DATE LETTER	LION PASSANT	
1776-77	👑	a	🦁	
1777-78	"	b	"	
1778-79	"	c	"	
1779-80	"	d	"	
1780-81	"	e	"	
1781-82	"	f	"	
1782-83	"	g	"	
1783-84	"	h	"	
Up to-30 Nov.1784	"	i	"	
				DUTY MARK
From 1 Dec. 1784-85*	"	"	"	👑
1785-86*	"	k	"	"
1786-87	"	l	"	👤
1787-88	"	m	"	"
1788-89	"	n	"	"
1789-90	"	o	"	"
1790-91	"	p	"	"
1791-92	"	q	"	"
1792-93	"	r	"	"
1793-94	"	s	"	"
1794-95	"	t	"	"
1795-96	"	u	"	"
BRITANNIA STANDARD SILVER			
	BRITANNIA	DATE LETTER	LION'S HEAD ERASED
Date as Above	🛡	As Above	🦁

CYCLE XVII

STERLING STANDARD SILVER & GOLD (22ct)			
	LEOPARD'S HEAD CROWNED	DATE LETTER	LION PASSANT*	DUTY MARK
1796-97	🂠	**A**	🦁	👤
Up to 5 July 1797	"	**B**	"	"
6 July 1797 to 28 May 1798	"	"	"	👤
1798-99	"	**C**	"	👤
1799-1800	"	**D**	"	"
1800-1	"	**E**	"	"
1801-2	"	**F**	"	"
1802-3	"	**G**	"	"
1803-4	"	**H**	"	"
Up to 10 Oct.1804	"	**I**	"	"
11 Oct. 1804 to 28 May 1805	"	"	"	👤
1805-6	"	**K**	"	👤
1806-7	"	**L**	"	"
1807-8	"	**M**	"	"
1808-9	"	**N**	"	"
1809-10	"	**O**	"	"
1810-11	"	**P**	"	"
1811-12	"	**Q**	"	"
1812-13	"	**R**	"	"
1813-14	"	**S**	"	"
1814-15	"	**T**	"	"
Up to 13 June 1815	"	**U**	"	"
14 June to 31 Aug. 1815	"	"	"	👤
1 Sept. 1815 to 28 May 1816	"	"	"	👤

BRITANNIA STANDARD				
	BRITANNIA	DATE LETTER	LION'S HEAD ERASED	DUTY MARK
Date as Left	🂠	As Left	🦁	👤

GOLD (18ct.) 1798 on				
	LEOPARD'S HEAD ERASED	DATE LETTER	CROWN † + 18	DUTY MARK
Date as Left	🂠	As Left	👑18	👤

†   An alternative for the Crown + 18   🂠 **18**

CYCLE XVIII

BRITANNIA STANDARD SILVER

	BRITANNIA	DATE LETTER	LION'S HEAD ERASED	DUTY MARK
Date as Right		As Right		

GOLD (18ct.)

	LEOPARD'S HEAD CROWNED	DATE LETTER	CROWN † + 18	DUTY MARK
Date as Right		As Right		

† An alternative for the Crown + 18

§ Added 1816-1843 for 22ct. gold.

STERLING STANDARD SILVER & GOLD (22ct)

	LEOPARD'S HEAD	DATE LETTER	LION* PASSANT	DUTY MARK
1816-17§		a		
1817-18	"	b	"	"
1818-19	"	c	"	"
1819-20	"	d	"	"
GEO.IV 1820-21	"	e	"	"
1821-22	"	f	"	"
		"		
1822-23	"	g	"	"
1823-24	"	h	"	"
1824-25	"	i	"	"
1825-26		k	"	"
1826-27		l	"	"
1827-28	"	m	"	"
1828-29	"	n	"	"
1829-30	"	o	"	"
WM.IV 1830-31	"	p	"	"
1831-32	"	q	"	"
1832-33	"	r	"	"
1833-34	"	s	"	"
1834-35	"	t	"	
1835-36	"	u	"	"

CYCLE XIX

STERLING STANDARD SILVER & GOLD (22ct)

	LEOPARD'S HEAD	DATE LETTER	LION PASSANT	DUTY MARK
1836-37	🦁	𝔄	🦁	👑
VICT. 29th May to 20th June 1837	"	𝔅	"	"
21st June 1837 to 28th May 1838	🦁	"	🦁	👑
1838-39	"	ℭ	"	"
1839-40	"	𝔇	"	👑
1840-41	🦁	𝔈	🦁	👑
1841-42	"	𝔉	"	"
1842-43	"	𝔊	"	"
1843-44	"	ℌ	"	"
1844-45	"	𝔍	"	"
1845-46	"	𝔎	"	"
1846-47	"	𝔏	"	"
1847-48	"	𝔐	"	"
1848-49	"	𝔑	"	"
1849-50	"	𝔒	"	"
1850-51	"	𝔓	"	"
1851-52	"	𝔔	"	"
1852-53	"	𝔕	"	"
1853-54	"	𝔖	"	"
1854-55	"	𝔗	"	"
1855-56	"	𝔘	"	"

BRITANNIA STANDARD SILVER

	BRITANNIA	DATE LETTER	LION'S HEAD ERASED	DUTY MARK
Date as Left	🛡	As Left	🦁	👑

GOLD (22ct.) 1844 ONWARDS

	LEOPARD'S HEAD	DATE LETTER	CROWN + 22	DUTY MARK
Date as Left	🦁	𝔍	👑 22	👑

GOLD (18ct.)

	LEOPARD'S HEAD	DATE LETTER	CROWN + 18	DUTY MARK
Date as Left	🦁	As Left	👑 18	👑

FROM 1854

GOLD (15ct.)

	LEOPARD'S HEAD	DATE LETTER	CARAT MARK	DUTY MARK
Date as Left	🦁	𝔘	15	·625	👑

GOLD (12ct.)

	LEOPARD'S HEAD	DATE LETTER	CARAT MARK	DUTY MARK
Date as Left	🦁	𝔘	12	·5	👑

GOLD (9ct.)

	LEOPARD'S HEAD	DATE LETTER	CARAT MARK	DUTY MARK
Date as Left	🦁	𝔘	9	·375	👑

† Variation: 👑 18

CYCLE XX

BRITANNIA STANDARD SILVER*

	LION'S HEAD ERASED	DATE LETTER	BRIT-ANNIA	DUTY MARK
Date as Right		As Right		

GOLD (22ct.)*

	LEOPARD'S HEAD	DATE LETTER	CROWN + 22	DUTY MARK
Date as Right			22	

GOLD (18ct.)*

	LEOPARD'S HEAD	DATE LETTER	CROWN + 18	DUTY MARK
Date as Right			18	

GOLD (15ct.)*

	LEOPARD'S HEAD	DATE LETTER	CARAT MARK	DUTY MARK
Date as Right			·625	

GOLD (12ct.)*

	LEOPARD'S HEAD	DATE LETTER	CARAT MARK	DUTY MARK
Date as Right			·5	

GOLD (9ct.)*

	LEOPARD'S HEAD	DATE LETTER	CARAT MARK	DUTY MARK
Date as Right			·375	

STERLING STANDARD SILVER*

	LEOPARD'S HEAD	DATE LETTER	LION PASSANT	DUTY MARK
1856-57		a		
1857-58	"	b	"	"
1858-59	"	c	"	"
1859-60	"	d	"	"
1860-61	"	e	"	"
1861-62	"	f	"	"
1862-63	"	g	"	"
1863-64	"	h	"	"
1864-65	"	i	"	"
1865-66	"	k	"	"
1866-67	"	l	"	"
1867-68	"	m	"	"
1868-69	"	n	"	"
1869-70	"	o	"	"
1870-71	"	p	"	"
1871-72	"	q	"	"
1872-73	"	r	"	"
1873-74	"	s	"	"
1874-75	"	t	"	"
1875-76	"	u	"	"

 was struck on imported wares in addition to the marks shown, from 1867-1904.

CYCLE XXI

STERLING STANDARD SILVER*

	LEOPARD'S HEAD	DATE LETTER	LION PASSANT	DUTY MARK
1876-77	(leopard's head)	**A**	(lion passant)	(duty mark)
1877-78	"	**B**	"	"
1878-79	"	**C**	"	"
1879-80	"	**D**	"	"
1880-81	"	**E**	"	"
1881-82	"	**F**	"	"
1882-83	"	**G**	"	"
1883-84	"	**H**	"	"
1884-85	"	**I**	"	"
1885-86	"	**K**	"	"
1886-87	"	**L**	"	"
1887-88	"	**M**	"	"
1888-89	"	**N**	"	"
1889-1st May 1890	"	**O**	"	"
2nd May 1890 28th May 1890	"	"	"	
June 1890-91	"	**P**	"	
1891-92	"	**Q**	"	
1892-93	"	**R**	"	
1893-94	"	**S**	"	
1894-95	"	**T**	"	
1895-96	"	**U**	"	

BRITANNIA STANDARD SILVER*

	LION'S HEAD	DATE LETTER	BRIT- ANNIA	DUTY MARK
Date as Left	(lion's head)	**A**	(britannia)	(duty mark)

GOLD (22ct.)*

	LEOPARD'S HEAD	DATE LETTER	CROWN + 22	DUTY MARK
Date as Left	(leopard's head)	**A**	(crown) **22**	(duty mark)

GOLD (18ct.)*

	LEOPARD'S HEAD	DATE LETTER	CROWN + 18	DUTY MARK
Date as Left	(leopard's head)	**A**	(crown 18)	(duty mark)

GOLD (15ct.)*

	LEOPARD'S HEAD	DATE LETTER	CARAT MARK	DUTY MARK
Date as Left	(leopard's head)	**A**	(15) **·625**	(duty mark)

GOLD (12ct.)*

	LEOPARD'S HEAD	DATE LETTER	CARAT MARK	DUTY MARK
Date as Left	(leopard's head)	**A**	(12) **·5**	(duty mark)

GOLD (9ct.)*

	LEOPARD'S HEAD	DATE LETTER	CARAT MARK	DUTY MARK
Date as Left	(leopard's head)	**A**	(9) **·375**	(duty mark)

* (F) was struck on imported wares in addition to the marks shown, from 1867-1904.

† Duty Mark only to 1890.

CYCLE XXII

BRITANNIA STANDARD SILVER*

	LION'S HEAD ERASED	DATE LETTER	BRITANNIA
Date as Right	🦁	As Right	🏛️

GOLD (22ct.)*

	LEOPARD'S HEAD ¦	CROWN + 22	DATE LETTER
Date as Right	🦁	👑 22	a

GOLD (18ct.)*

	LEOPARD'S HEAD ¦	CROWN + 18 ‡	DATE LETTER
Date as Right	🦁	👑18	a

GOLD (15ct.)*

	LEOPARD'S HEAD	CARAT MARK	DATE LETTER
Date as Right	🦁	15·625	a

GOLD (12ct.)*

	LEOPARD'S HEAD	CARAT MARK	DATE LETTER
Date as Right	🦁	12·5	a

GOLD (9ct.)*

	LEOPARD'S HEAD	CARAT MARK	DATE LETTER
Date as Right	🦁	9·375	a

STERLING STANDARD SILVER*

	LEOPARD'S HEAD	DATE LETTER	LION PASSANT
1896-97	🦁	a	🦁
1897-98	"	b	"
1898-99	"	c	"
1899-1900	"	d	"
1900-1	"	e	"
EDW.VII 1901-2	"	f	"
1902-3	"	g	"
1903-4	"	h	"
1904-5	"	i	"
1905-6	"	k	"
1906-7	"	l	"
1907-8	"	m	"
1908-9	"	n	"
1909-10	"	o	"
GEO.V 1910-11	"	p	"
1911-12	"	q	"
1912-13	"	r	"
1913-14	"	s	"
1914-15	"	t	"
1915-16	"	u	"

* was struck on imported wares in addition to the marks shown from 1867-1904.

¦ replaces previous Leopard's Head shown, from 1897-98.

‡ Alternative mark up to 1904. From 1904 onwards only separate punches Crown and 18 used.

CYCLE XXII (continued)

IMPORTED WARES	
1904-1905 ⊛	1906 on ⊕
Silver (Britannia) 9584	🅸
,, (Sterling) 925	🅸
Gold 22ct. 22 916	🅸
,, 18ct. 18 ·75	🅸
,, 15ct. 15 ·625	🅸
,, 12ct. 12 ·5	🅸
,, 9ct. ·375	🅸

CYCLE XXIII**

BRITANNIA STANDARD SILVER			
	LION'S HEAD ERASED	BRIT-ANNIA	DATE LETTER
Date as Right			As Right

GOLD (22ct.)			
	LEOPARD'S HEAD	CARAT MARK	DATE LETTER
Date as Right		22	a

GOLD (18ct.)			
	LEOPARD'S HEAD	CARAT MARK	DATE LETTER
Date as Right		18	a

GOLD (15ct.) up to 1932 †			
	LEOPARD'S HEAD	CARAT MARK	DATE LETTER
Date as Right		15 ·625	a

GOLD (12ct.) up to 1932 †			
	LEOPARD'S HEAD	CARAT MARK	DATE LETTER
Date as Right		12 ·5	a

GOLD (9ct.)			
	LEOPARD'S HEAD	CARAT MARK	DATE LETTER
Date as Right		·375	a

STERLING STANDARD SILVER			
	LEOPARD'S HEAD	LION PASSANT	DATE LETTER
1916-17			a
1917-18	"	"	b
1918-19	"	"	c
1919-20	"	"	d
1920-21	"	"	e
1921-22	"	"	f
1922-23	"	"	g
1923-24			h
1924-25	"	"	i
1925-26	"	"	k
1926-27	"	"	l
1927-28	"	"	m
1928-29	"	"	n
1929-30	"	"	o
1930-31	"	"	p
1931-32	"	"	q
1932-33	"	"	r
1933-34	"	"	s
*1934-35	"	"	t
*1935-36	"	"	u

GOLD (14ct.) from 1932 †			
	LEOPARD'S HEAD	CARAT MARK	DATE LETTER
Date as Right		14 ·585	r

* Jubilee mark. This was a voluntary mark used in these years.

† 12ct. and 15ct. gold were discontinued in 1932-33 and replaced by a single standard, 14ct. gold.

** For import marks Cycle XXIII see p.42.

CYCLE XXIV**

STERLING STANDARD SILVER		
LEOPARD'S HEAD	LION PASSANT	DATE LETTER
EDW.VII 1936-37	🐆	🦁	**A**
GEO.VI 1937-38	"	"	**B**
1938-39	"	"	**C**
1939-40	"	"	**D**
1940-41	"	"	**E**
1941-42	"	"	**F**
1942-43	"	"	**G**
1943-44	"	"	**H**
1944-45	"	"	**I**
1945-46	"	"	**K**
1946-47	"	"	**L**
1947-48	"	"	**M**
1948-49	"	"	**N**
1949-50	"	"	**O**
1950-51	"	"	**P**
1951-52	"	"	**Q**
ELIZ.II 1952-53*	"	"	**R**
1953-54*	"	"	**S**
1954-55	"	"	**T**
1955-56	"	"	**U**

BRITANNIA STANDARD SILVER		
LION'S HEAD ERASED	BRIT-ANNIA	DATE LETTER
Date as Left	🛡	🦁	As Left

GOLD (22ct.)			
LEOPARD'S HEAD	CARAT MARK		DATE LETTER
Date as Left	🦁	👑	22	**A**

GOLD (18ct.)			
LEOPARD'S HEAD	CARAT MARK		DATE LETTER
Date as Left	🦁	👑	18	**A**

GOLD (14ct.)			
LEOPARD'S HEAD	CARAT MARK		DATE LETTER
Date as Left	🦁	♔ ·585		**A**

GOLD (9ct.)			
LEOPARD'S HEAD	CARAT MARK		DATE LETTER
Date as Left	🦁	◈ ·375		**A**

*   🙂 A coronation mark was also used in these years as an optional additional mark.

**   For import marks Cycle XXIV see p.42.

CYCLE XXV**

BRITANNIA STANDARD SILVER

	LION'S HEAD ERASED	BRIT-ANNIA	DATE LETTER
Date as Right			As Right

GOLD (22ct.)

	LEOPARD'S HEAD	CARAT MARK	DATE LETTER
Date as Right		22	a

GOLD (18ct.)

	LEOPARD'S HEAD	CARAT MARK	DATE LETTER
Date as Right		18	a

GOLD (14ct.)

	LEOPARD'S HEAD	CARAT MARK	DATE LETTER
Date as Right		·585	a

GOLD (9ct.)

	LEOPARD'S HEAD	CARAT MARK	DATE LETTER
Date as Right		·375	a

** For import marks Cycle XXV see p.42.

STERLING STANDARD SILVER

	LEOPARD'S HEAD	LION PASSANT	DATE LETTER
1956-57			a
1957-58	"	"	b
1958-59	"	"	c
1959-60	"	"	d
1960-61	"	"	e
1961-62	"	"	f
1962-63	"	"	g
1963-64	"	"	h
1964-65	"	"	i
1965-66	"	"	k
1966-67	"	"	l
1967-68	"	"	m
1968-69	"	"	n
1969-70	"	"	o
1970-71	"	"	p
1971-72	"	"	q
1972-73	"	"	r
1973-74	"	"	s
Up to 31 Dec.1974	"	"	t

CYCLES XXIII, XXIV & XXV

MARKS ON IMPORTED WARES

	IMPORT MARK †	CARAT MARK	DATE LETTER
Silver (Britannia)	♌	9584	𝖆
Silver (Sterling)	♌	925	𝖆
Gold 22ct.	♌	⅗ 916	𝖆
" 18ct.	♌	⅔ 75	𝖆
" 15ct.*	♌	⅝ ·625	𝖆
" 12ct.*	♌	⬥ ·5	𝖆
" 9ct.	♌	⬥ ·375	𝖆

MARKS ON IMPORTED WARES* (From 1932)

	IMPORT MARK †	CARAT MARK	DATE LETTER
Gold 14ct.	♌	⬥ 585	𝖗

*   12ct. and 15ct. gold were discontinued in 1932-33 and replaced by a single standard, 14ct. gold.

†   From 1950 on the import (Leo) mark is struck the other way up.

CYCLE XXVI

STERLING STANDARD SILVER

	LEOPARD'S HEAD	LION PASSANT	DATE LETTER
1975	🦁	🦁	𝓐
1976	"	"	𝓑
1977*	"	"	𝓒
1978	"	"	𝓓
1979	"	"	𝓔
1980	"	"	𝓕
1981	"	"	𝓖
1982	"	"	𝓗
1983	"	"	𝓘
1984	"	"	𝓚
1985	"	"	𝓛
1986	"	"	𝓜
1987	"	"	𝓝
1988	"	"	𝓞
1989	"	"	𝓟
1990	"	"	𝓠
1991	"	"	𝓡

BRITANNIA STANDARD SILVER

	LEOPARD'S HEAD	BRITANNIA	DATE LETTER
Date as Above	🦁	🦁	𝓐

PLATINUM

	LEOPARD'S HEAD	PLATINUM MARK	DATE LETTER
Date as Above	🦁	⬠	𝓐

GOLD

	LEOPARD'S HEAD	CARAT MARK		DATE LETTER
22ct.	🦁	👑	916	𝓐
18ct.	🦁	⚖	750	𝓐
14ct.	🦁	⚖	585	𝓐
9ct.	🦁	👑	375	𝓐

* Silver Jubilee mark (optional)

CYCLE XXVI (continued)

IMPORT MARKS			
	IMPORT MARK	CARAT MARK	DATE LETTER
Silver (Britannia)	෴	958	𝓐
Silver (Sterling)	෴	925	𝓐
Gold 22ct.	෴	916	𝓐
„ 18ct.	෴	750	𝓐
„ 14ct.	෴	585	𝓐
„ 9ct.	෴	375	𝓐
Platinum	෴	950	𝓐

CONVENTION HALLMARKS

PRECIOUS METAL	LEOPARD'S HEAD	COMMON CONTROL MARK	FINENESS MARK
Gold 18ct.	(leopard's head)	750	750
14ct.	"	585	585
9ct.	"	375	375
Silver (Sterling)	"	925	925
Platinum	"	950	950

ON IMPORTED WARES

PRECIOUS METAL	IMPORT MARK	COMMON CONTROL MARK	FINENESS MARK
Gold 18ct.	(import mark)	750	750
14ct.	"	585	585
9ct.	"	375	375
Silver (Sterling)	(import mark)	925	925
Platinum	(import mark)	950	950

Marks reproduced courtesy The Worshipful Company of Goldsmiths.

MARK	MAKER	PERIOD	COMMENTS
A&CºLᵀᴰ	Asprey & Co Ltd	This mark early 20th C on	Justifiably famous for the quality of its products
AB	Abraham Buteux - post 1721 sterling mark	2nd ¼ 18th C	Fine Huguenot maker
AB GB	Alice & George Burrows	Early 19th C	Good, run-of-the-mill makers
A	Adie Brothers Ltd	20th C	Prolific makers
A·B·S	A B Savory	2nd ¼ 19th C	Large 19th C firm
A·C	Ann Chesterman	Last ¼ 18th C	Mainly small pieces of holloware
AC	Augustine Courtauld	1st ½ 18th C	Fine Huguenot maker, quite prolific
AC	" "	" "	
A·C	Alexander Crichton	Late 19th/20th C	Usually very fine copies of earlier pieces
ACºₒₜᵈ	The Alexander Clark Co Ltd	1st ½ 19th C	Prolific manufacturers
AC MCº	The Alexander Clark Manufacturing Co		
AD	Alfred Dunhill	20th C	Usually smokers' accessories
AF	Alexander Field	Late 18th/Early 19th C	Run-of-the-mill work (do not confuse with Andrew Fogelberg)
A·F	Andrew Fogelberg	2nd ½ 18th C	Very important and interesting work (do not confuse this mark with that of Alexander Field, whose work is quite inferior. The period of overlap is 1780-93, during which period Fogelberg was in partner-ship with Gilbert, using the AF SG mark)
A·F S·G / AF SG	Andrew Fogelberg & Stephen Gilbert	Last ¼ 18th C	Very important and interesting work
AL / AL	Thomas Allen	Late 17th/Early 18th C	Spoon maker
A·L / AL	Aug. Le Sage	2nd ½ 18th C	Important maker

MARK	MAKER	PERIOD	COMMENTS
AP	Abraham Portal	3rd ¼ 18th C	Apprentice to Paul de Lamerie but shows none of his master's flair. He was more interested in drama!
AR	Peter Archambo I	1st ½ 18th C	Important Huguenot
A·P·O	Hugh Arnett & Edward Pocock	c.2nd ¼ 18th C	Wide range, a lot of flatware
AS·CD·LD	The Artificer's Guild Ltd	1st ½ 20th C	Interesting art metalwork
AS JS AS	Adey, Joseph & Albert Savory	Mid 19th C	Large 19th c family firm
AT	Anne Tanqueray	2nd ¼ 18th C	Probably the greatest of all women silversmiths
AV	Ayme Videau	2nd ¼ 18th C	Fine Huguenot maker of particularly good coffee pots
AV	" "	" "	
AZJZ	Arthur Zimmerman & John Zimmerman	Late 19th/Early 20th C	Prolific manufacturers of cigarette cases, boxes, vesta cases, etc.
Ba	Thomas Bamford	c.2nd ¼ 18th C	Prolific maker of good, run-of-the-mill casters
BA	Joseph Barbut	1st ¼ 18th C	Spoon maker
BA	Richard Bayley	1st ½ 18th C	Prolific maker of good holloware
BD	Burrage Davenport	2nd ½ 18th C	Good, run-of-the-mill work
BE	Benjamin Bentley	Late 17th/Early 18th C	Spoon maker
B·G	Benjamin Godfrey	2nd ¼ 18th C	A very fine goldsmith
P·G	" "	" "	
BG	" "	" "	
B.H.M	Berthold Hermann Muller	Late 19th/Early 20th C	Importer of vast quantities of silver from Germany, based on earlier work (much collected today)
BI	Joseph Bird	Late 17th/Early 18th C	Mostly good candlesticks
Bi	" "	" "	
BM	Berthold Muller	Late 19th/Early 20th C	Importer of vast quantities of silver from Germany, based on earlier work (much collected today)
BM	" "	" "	

MARK	MAKER	PERIOD	COMMENTS
John Bodington	John Bodington	Late 17th/Early 18th C	Very fine English work. One of the best English goldsmiths of the period
	Jonathan Bradley	Late 17th/Early 18thC	Spoon maker
BS	Benjamin Smith	1st ¼ 19th C	Important maker (part of Rundell, Bridge & Rundell)
BS IS	Benjamin & James Smith	Early 19th C	Highly important (worked for Rundell, Bridge & Rundell)
	Abraham Buteux	2nd ¼ 18th C	Fine Huguenot maker
	Benjamin Watts - post 1720 sterling mark	Late 17th/Early 18th C	Mostly spoons
C&Cº	Carrington & Co	20th C	Retailers, often fine reproductions
C&C	Collingwood & Co	20th C	Retailers
C&WPᵗ	Charles Padgett & Walter Padgett	Early 20th C	Became Padgett & Braham; very large producer today
Co	Lawrence Coles	Late 17th/Early 18th C	Spoon maker
CA	Charles Asprey	Mid 19th C	Justifiably famous for the quality of its products
C.A C.A	Charles Asprey & Charles Asprey jun	End 19th C	
CA·GA	Charles Asprey & George Asprey	Late 19th/Early 20th C	
CA	Christopher Canner I	Late 17th/Early 18th C	Many casters
C·A	Charles Aldridge & Henry Green	2nd ½ 18th C	Good, run-of-the-mill work
C.B	Charles Belk	Late 19th/Early 20th C	Manufacturer
CB	Charles Bellassyse	Mid 18th C	Good maker
C·B	Charles Boyton	Mid 19th C	Spoon maker
CB	" "	2nd ½ 19th C	Spoon maker and manufacturer of a wide range
CB	" "	End 19th C	
C&B S	Charles Boyton & Son	20th C	

MARK	MAKER	PERIOD	COMMENTS
	Christopher Canner - post 1720 sterling mark	Late 17th/Early 18th C	Many casters
	Charles Eley	2nd ¼ 19th C	Spoon maker
	Charles Fabergé	Early 20th C	London branch of the famous Peter Carl Fabergé of St. Petersburg
	Charles Thomas Fox	1st ½ 19th C	Member of an important 19th C family of goldsmiths
	" "	" "	
	Crispin Fuller	1st ¼ 19th C	Run-of-the-mill maker
	Charles Frederick Hancock	2nd ½ 19th C	Important makers and retailers
	" "	" "	
	" "	" "	
	Hancocks & Co	Late 19th C & on	
	" "	" "	
	Carlo Giuliano	2nd ½ 19th C	Important jeweller
	Carlo Joseph Giuliano & Arthur Alphonse Giuliano	Late 19th/Early 20th C	Important jewellers
	Wm Charnelhouse	Early 18th C	Often found on spoons
	John Chartier	Late 17th/Early 18th C	Very important Huguenot
	" "	" "	
	Christian Hillan	2nd ¼ 18th C	A very fine maker
	Charles Hougham	Last ¼ 18th C	Usually spoons and buckles
	Charles Kandler	Mid 18th C	Highly important, one of the all-time greats

MARK	MAKER	PERIOD	COMMENTS
CK	Charles Kandler II	Last ¼ 18th C	Do not confuse with the highly important Charles Frederick Kandler
CL	Jos Clare	1st ¼ 18th C	Good prolific maker, wide range
CL	Nicholas Clausen	1st ¼ 18th C	Important and interesting maker. Work is difficult to find
CL	David Clayton	Late 17th/Early 18th C	Specialist toy and miniature maker. Very collectable
CL	Jonah Clifton	Early 18th C	Good holloware
CM	Charles Mappin	Late 19th C	Manufacturer
Co	Matt Cooper	Early 18th C	Mostly fine candlesticks
CO	Robert Cooper	Late 17th/Early 18th C	Made pieces for Samuel Pepys. Good English maker
CO	Edward Cornock	1st ¼ 18th C	Mostly small salvers, spoon trays and tobacco boxes
CO	John Corporon	1st ¼ 18th C	Very fine Huguenot work, but difficult to find
CO	Augustus Courtauld	1st ½ 18th C	Quite prolific. Fine Huguenot maker
CR	Paul Crespin	Mid 18th C	Highly important, and serious rival to Paul de Lamerie, certainly his equal
CR	" "	" "	
CR	" "	" "	
CR A	Charles Robert Ashbee	Late 19th/Early 20th C	Very important Arts & Crafts
CR GS	Charles Reily & George Storer	2nd ¼ 19th C	Very fine small work
CR WS	Charles Rawlings & William Summers	Mid 19th C	Fine and very collectable small work
CS✱FS	Cornelius Desormeaux Saunders & James Francis Hollings Shepherd	Late 19th/Early 20th C	Prolific manufacturers of small work and jewellery
CS FS	Cornelius Saunders & Frank Shepherd	Late 19th/Early 20th C	Prolific manufacturers of small work and jewellery

MARK	MAKER	PERIOD	COMMENTS
CSH	Charles Stuart Harris	2nd ½ 19th C	Spoon maker
CSH	" "	" "	
C.S H	" "	Late 19th/Early 20th C	Prolific maker of a very wide range, usually very fine copies of earlier pieces
C S &S	C S Harris & Sons Ltd	Late 19th/Early 20th C	
C.S.H&s	" "	" "	
CTF GF	Charles Thomas Fox & George Fox	Mid 19th C	Important makers
CV	Louys Cuny	1st ¼ 18th C	Very fine Huguenot
C W	Charles Wright	3rd ¼ 18th C	Good standard holloware
D&J W	D & J Wellby Ltd	2nd ½ 19th C/c.20th C	Mostly fine copies of early pieces
DA	Isaac Dalton	1st ¼ 18th C	Spoon maker
DA	Wm Darker	1st ½ 18th C	Good general maker, quite prolific
DA	Isaac Davenport	Late 17th/Early 18th C	Spoon maker
DB	David Clayton - post 1720 sterling mark	Late 17th/Early 18th C	Specialist toy/miniature maker. Very collectable
DH	David Hennell	Mid 18th C	Specialist and prolific maker of salts
D·H	" "	" "	
D·H	" "	" "	
R D·H H	D & R Hennell	3rd ¼ 18th C	Mostly salts
DI	Isaac Dighton	Late 17th/Early 18th C	Good English work of the period
DM	Dorothy Mills	Mid 18th C	Good, usually small pieces
D·P	Daniel Piers	Mid 18th C	Fine maker
DP	" "	" "	

MARK	MAKER	PERIOD	COMMENTS
DS BS / **DS BS IS**	Digby Scott & Benjamin Smith / Digby Scott, Benjamin Smith & James Smith	Early 19th C	Highly important (worked for Rundell, Bridge & Rundell)
DS RS / **R DS S** / **DS RS**	Daniel Smith & Robert Sharp / " " / " "	2nd ½ 18th C / " " / Last ¼ 18th C	Important makers. Made some of the finest silver of the period
DT	David Tanqueray - post 1720 sterling mark	1st ¼ 18th C	Very fine Huguenot work associated with his father-in-law, David Willaume
DU NH	Duncan Urquhart & Naphtali Hart	Late 18th/Early 19th C	Run-of-the-mill tea services
DW	David Willaume - post 1720 sterling mark	Late 17th/Early 18th C	Very important Huguenot
DW / **DW**	David Willaume II / " "	2nd ¼ 18th C / " "	Important Huguenot
DW JW / **DW JW** / **DWJW**	Daniel & John Wellby / " " / " "	2nd ½ 19th C/c.20th C / " " / " "	Mostly fine copies of early pieces
E&Co / **ECoLD**	Elkington & Co Ltd (of Birmingham) / " "	Mid 19th/20th C / " "	Major manufacturer whose work ranges from the very ordinary to very important designs; the quality is always superb
EA	John East	Late 17th/Early 18th C	Good English maker
EA / **EA A** / **EA**	Edward Aldridge / Edward Aldridge & Co / Edward Aldridge & John Stamper	Mid 18th C / 3rd ¼ 18th C	Good, run-of-the-mill maker, mostly pierced work, baskets, etc.

MARK	MAKER	PERIOD	COMMENTS
	Elizabeth Buteux	2nd ¼ 18th C	One of the best women silversmiths
	Edward, Edward jun, John & William Barnard	2nd ¼ 19th C	Major manufacturers
	Edward Barnard & John Barnard	Mid 19th C	
	" "	" "	
	Edward, John & William Barnard	" "	
	Edward Barnard & Sons Ltd	Early 20th C	
	Ebenezer Coker	Mid 18th C	Specialist in spoons, salvers and candlesticks (often confused with Elias Cachart, look at loops at end of letters: Cachart loops back through, Coker does not)
	" "	" "	
	Edw Cornock - post 1723 sterling mark	1st ¼ 18th C	Mostly small salvers, spoon trays and tobacco boxes
	Elizabeth Eaton	Mid 19th C	Specialist spoon maker
	" "	" "	
	Elizabeth Eaton & John Eaton	" "	
	Edward Farrell	1st ½ 19th C	Very interesting maker, producing important if at times eccentric (today very valuable) pieces
	Edward Feline	Late 1st ¼/2nd ¼ 18th C	Fine work, many good coffee pots
	" "	" "	
	Elizabeth Godfrey	Mid 18th C	One of the best women silversmiths (formerly Elizabeth Buteux, see entry)
	Edward Hutton (Wm Hutton & Sons)	2nd ½ 19th C/20th C	Large Sheffield manufacturers
	Elizabeth Jackson (later Oldfield)	Mid 18th C	Specialist spoon maker
	Edward Ker Reid	2nd ½ 19th C	Good general work
	Elizabeth Morley	Late 18th C	Small pieces

MARK	MAKER	PERIOD	COMMENTS
EM JM	Edward Mappin & Joseph C Mappin	2nd ½ 19th C	Large Sheffield manufacturers
E O	Elizabeth Oldfield (formerly Jackson)	3rd ¼ 18th C	Specialist spoon maker
E R	Elizabeth Roker	Last ¼ 18th C	Spoon maker
E R	Emick Romer	3rd ¼ 18th C	Interesting maker who often made epergnes
E T E·T	Elizabeth Tookey " "	3rd ¼ 18th C " "	Spoon maker
E·V EV	Edward Vincent " "	1st ½ 18th C " "	Very fine English craftsman, who could be naughty; he was into duty dodging after 1720 in a big way: be careful
EW	Edward Wakelin	3rd ¼ 18th C	Very important maker
EW EW	Edward Wood " "	2nd ¼ 18th C " "	Specialist salt maker
F	Wm Fawdery - pre-1697 and post 1720 sterling mark	Late 17th/Early 18th C	Good English work
FA	William Fawdery	" "	
FA	Wm Fawdery	" "	
FA	" "	" "	
FA	John Fawdery	1st ¼ 18th C	Good holloware
FA	Thos Farren	1st ½ 18th C	Very fine maker
F·B ND	Francis Butty & Nich Dumee	3rd ¼ 18th C	Good makers
FBT	Francis Boone Thomas (F B Thomas & Co)	2nd ½ 19th C/1st ½ 20th C	Bond Street retailer (always fine quality pieces)
FC	Fras Crump	Mid 18th C	Good maker of fairly standard holloware
F·C	" "	" "	
FC	" "	" "	

MARK	MAKER	PERIOD	COMMENTS
Frederick Elkington	Frederick Elkington	Mid 19th/20th C	Major manufacturers whose work ranges from the very ordinary to very important designs; the quality is always superb
	Francis Garthorne – pre-1697 and post 1721 sterling mark	Late 17th/Early 18th C	Competent English work of the period
	Fras Higgins I	1st ½ 19th C	Important 19th C spoon maker
	Francis Higgins	Mid 19th C	Specialist spoon maker
	" "	" "	
	" "	" "	
	" "	2nd ½ 19th/Early 20th C	
	" "	" "	
	F Higgins & Son Ltd	Early 20th C	
	Charles Frederick Kandler	Mid 18th C	Highly important, one of the all-time greats
	" "	" "	
	Fred Knopfell	3rd ¼ 18th C	Very interesting former journeyman of Paul de Lamerie
	Wm Fleming	c.1st ¼ 18th C	Very prolific, particularly peppers, saucepans and mugs
	Francis Nelme	c.2nd ¼ 18th C	Important, but over-shadowed by his father
	" "	" "	
	Thos Folkingham	c.1st ¼ 18th C	Wide range of fine silver
	Fras Stamp	Last ¼ 18th C	Good maker
	Fuller White	Mid 18th C	Good, run-of-the-mill holloware
	" "	" "	

MARK	MAKER	PERIOD	COMMENTS
	Fuller White & John Fray	Mid 18th C	Good holloware
	Goldsmiths & Silver-smiths Co Ltd	20th C	Very large retailers of jewellery and silver
	" "	" "	
	" "	" "	
	Daniel Garnier	Late 17th/Early 18th C	Important Huguenot
	George W Adams (Chawner & Co)	Mid 19th C	Chawners were the most important mid 19th C firm of spoon makers
	George Angell	Mid 19th C	Important maker
	" "	" "	
	William Gamble	Late 17th/Early 18th C	Competent English maker - Hogarth was apprenticed to his son
	Geo Garthorne	Late 17th/Early 18th C	Competent English work of the period
	George Burrows	2nd ½ 18th C	Usually spoons
	George Cowles	Late 18th C	Good maker
	George Fox	2nd ½ 19th C	Member of the important Fox family
	" "	" "	
	George Gray	Last ¼ 18th C	Often overstruck on the work of Hester Bateman and Peter and Ann Bateman
	George Hindmarsh	Mid 18th C	Specialist salver maker
	" "	" "	
	George Heming & William Chawner	Last ¼ 18th C	Fine makers
	" "	" "	

MARK	MAKER	PERIOD	COMMENTS
	Glover Johnson - post 1720 sterling mark	1st ¼ 18th C	Prolific maker of ordinary casters
	George Greenhill Jones	2nd ¼ 18th C	Mostly casters and sauce-pans
	George Jackson & David Fullerton	Very end 19th/Early 20th C	Wide range, particularly good flatware
	George Lambert	2nd ½ 19th C	Fine maker
	Gilbert Marks	Late 19th/Early 20th C	Important art nouveau work
	George Methuen	Mid 18th C	Specialist in salvers, etc.
	" "	" "	
	Gorham Manu-facturing Co	20th C	Large American manu-facturer with Birmingham factory
	George Maudsley Jackson	Late 19th C	Wide range of particularly good flatware
	George Nathan & Ridley Hayes	Late 19th/Early 20th C	Birmingham manu-facturers
	Meshach Godwin	Late 1st/2nd ¼ 18th C	Mostly run-of-the-mill peppers and other small pieces
	James Gould	Late 1st/2nd ¼ 18th C	Specialist candlestick maker
	William Gould	Mid 18th C	Specialist candlestick maker
	Jas Goodwin	1st ¼ 18th C	Small mugs, peppers, etc.
	George Henry Hart (Guild of Handicraft)	1908 and on	Formed by members of the Guild of Handicraft Ltd after its liquidation (Note: do not confuse with next mark which it resembles. From 1912 on it is George Hart)
	Guild of Handicraft Ltd	1900-1908	Important Arts & Crafts makers under C R Ashbee. (Note: easy to confuse with George Hart's mark above. Date is important and look for the Ltd after the G of H)
	David Greene	1st ¼ 18th C	Specialist candlestick maker

MARK	MAKER	PERIOD	COMMENTS
GR	Henry Greene	Early 18th C	Mostly spoons
GR	Gundry Roode - post 1720 sterling mark	2nd ¼ 18th C	Salts
GRE	George Richards Elkington	Mid 19th/20th C	Major manufacturers whose work ranges from ordinary to very important designs; the quality is always superb
GS	Gabriel Sleath	1st ½ 18th C	Prolific, good English work
GS	" " - post 1720 sterling mark	" "	
GS	" " "	" "	
GS	George Smith III	Last ¼ 18th C	Prolific specialist spoon maker
GS	George Smith IV	Last ¼ 18th C	Prolific spoon maker
GSC	Gabriel Sleath & Fras Crump	Mid 18th C	Good, run-of-the-mill holloware
GS TH	George Smith & Thomas Hayter	Late 18th C	Good, general makers
GS TH	" "	" "	
GS WF	George Smith & William Fearn	Last ¼ 18th C	Prolific spoon makers
GU	Nathaniel Gulliver	2nd ¼ 18th C	Good holloware, particularly coffee pots
GU	George R Unite (of Birmingham)	Late 19th/Early 20th C	Prolific maker of small pieces
GW	George Wickes	Mostly 2nd ¼ 18th C	Very important English goldsmith
GW	" "	" "	
GW	" " - post 1721 sterling mark	" "	
GW	George Wintle	1st ¼ 19th C	Spoon maker
GW	" "	" "	
H&Co LD	Heming & Co Ltd (now Bruford & Heming)	20th C	Important retailers of silver and jewellery

MARK	MAKER	PERIOD	COMMENTS
	Hukin & Heath Ltd - 20th C mark	Late 19th/Early 20th C	Most important for their pieces designed by Dr C Dresser
	Hunt & Roskell Ltd	Late 19th C	Major 19th C firm, originates with Paul Storr
	" "	Early 20th C	
	Paul Hanet	1st/2nd ¼ 18th C	Huguenot spoonmaker
	Pierre Harache I	Late 17th C	Extremely important Huguenot
	Holland, Aldwinckle & Slater	Late 19th/Early 20th C	Important manufacturers
	" "	" "	
	Hugh Arnett & Edward Pocock - post 1720 sterling mark	c. 2nd ¼ 18th C	Wide range, a lot of flatware
	Henry Bailey	3rd ¼ 18th C	Standard commercial pieces
	" "	" "	(Note: this mark is often confused with that of Hester Bateman (see entry). The H does not flow with this mark as it does with Hester's)
	Hester Bateman	2nd ½ 18th C	Overrated, overpriced, run-of-the-mill, mass-produced pieces (see also Hy. Bailey re possible confusion with mark)
	" "	" "	
	Henry Brind	Mid 18th C	Good, run-of-the-mill maker
	Henry Chawner	Last ¼ 18th C	Run-of-the-mill maker
	Henry Chawner & Jno Eames	Late 18th C	Good, general work
	" "	" "	
	Henry Greenway	Last ¼ 18th C	A very good maker of particularly fine coffee pots, etc.
	Henry George Murphy	1st ½ 20th C	One of the most interesting Art Deco silversmiths

MARK	MAKER	PERIOD	COMMENTS
	Henry Hebert	2nd ¼ 18th C	Good maker
	" "	" "	
	" "	" "	
	" "	" "	
	" "	" "	
	Henry Holland (of Holland, Aldwinckle & Slater)	Mid 19th C	Important manufacturer
	" "	" "	
	Saml Hitchcock	1st ¼ 18th C	Spoon maker
	Henry John Lias	Late 19th C	Large manufacturing silversmith
	Henry John Lias & James Wakely	Late 19th C	Large manufacturing silversmith
	Herbert Charles Lambert (see Lambert & Rawlings)	Early 20th C	Important retailers
	Henry John Lias & Henry John Lias	Mid 19th C	Large manufacturing silversmith
	Hannah Northcote	1st ¼ 19th C	Spoon maker
	Henry Nutting & Robert Hennell	Early 19th C	Good makers
	Edward Holaday	1st ¼ 18th C	Good English work
	Sarah Holaday	Late 1st ¼/2nd ¼ 18th C	Good woman silversmith
	Humph Payne - post 1720 sterling mark	1st ½ 18th C	Good English work, quite prolific
	" "	" "	
	Harold Stabler	1st ½ 20th C	Important Art Deco work

MARK	MAKER	PERIOD	COMMENTS
HV AV	Henry Vander & Arthur Vander (now C J Vander Ltd)	Early 20th C	Important manufacturing silversmiths
HW &Cº HW &CºLᴰ	Henry Wilkinson & Co	Late 19th/Early 20th C	Important Sheffield manufacturers
I.S	James Schruder	Mid 18th C	Very fine maker who produced very interesting rococo
IA	Chas Jackson	1st ¼ 18th C	Spoon maker
I·B	Joseph Barbut - post 1720 sterling mark	1st ¼ 18th C	Spoon maker
I·B I·B	John Bridge " "	c. 2nd ¼ 19th C " "	Important maker (the Bridge of Rundell, Bridge & Rundell)
I·C I·C	Isaac Callard " "	2nd ¼ 18th C " "	Specialist spoon maker (good quality)
I·C	John Carter II	2nd ½ 18th C	Specialist candlestick and salver maker (Note: some of his candlesticks were designed by Robert Adam)
I·C	John Chartier - post 1723 sterling mark	Late 17th/Early 18th C	Very important Huguenot
I·C	Joseph Clare - post 1720 sterling mark	1st ¼ 18th C	Good, prolific maker, wide range
I·C T·H	John Crouch I & Thomas Hannam	2nd ½ 18th C	Very good makers
I·C WR	Joseph Craddock & William Reid	Early 19th C	Good makers
I·e	Thos Jenkins	Late 17th/Early 18th C	Important English maker
I·F	John Figg	Mid 19th C	Very fine and often interesting work
I·G I·G	James Gould - post 1721 sterling mark " "	Late 1st/2nd ¼ 18th C " "	Specialist candlestick maker
I H & R R I H & R R	John Hunt & Robert Roskell (mid to end 19th C marks)	Late 19th C	Major 19th C firm, originates with Paul Storr

MARK	MAKER	PERIOD	COMMENTS
I·J·K	John James Keith	Mid 19th C	Most prolific maker of church plate
I·K	John Keith	Mid 19th C	
I·K	" "	" "	
I·K R·S	John Keith & Richard Stiff	2nd ½ 19th C	
I·L	John Lambe	Last ¼ 18th C	Spoon maker
IL	Isaac Liger - post 1720 sterling mark	1st ¼ 18th C	Fine Huguenot pieces sometimes engraved by Simon Gribelin, in which case, very important
I·L H·L	John & Henry Lias	1st ½ 19th C	One of the most prolific 19th C family firms
H HL	" "	Mid 19th C	
I L HL CL	John, Henry & Charles Lias	c. 2nd ¼ 19th C	One of the most prolific 19th C family firms
I·M	Jacob Margas - post 1720 sterling mark	1st ¼ 18th C	Good Huguenot
IM	John Mewburn	Late 18th/Early 19th C	Good general work
I·M	Jno Millington - post 1720 sterling mark	1st ½ 18th C	Spoon maker
I & M ISH / **I & M ISH**	John Mortimer & John Samuel Hunt	Mid 19th C	Major 19th C firm, originates with Paul Storr
IM CK	Jas Murray & Chas Kandler	Mid 18th C	Kandler is highly important, one of the all-time greats. Little is known of Murray
IO	Glover Johnson	1st ¼ 18th C	Prolific maker of ordinary casters
IO	George Greenhill Jones	1st ½ 18th C	Mostly small pieces, peppers, cream jugs, etc.
IP	John Pollock	Mid 18th C	Good, run-of-the-mill maker
IP	Joseph Preedy	Late 18th/Early 19th C	Good maker
I·P E·W	John Parker & Edward Wakelin	3rd ¼ 18th C	Important makers
IR	Isaac Ribouleau - post 1720 sterling mark	2nd ¼ 18th C	Fine Huguenot, but difficult to find
IS	John Hugh le Sage	1st ½ 18th C	Important Huguenot gold-smith

MARK	MAKER	PERIOD	COMMENTS
I·S	John Scofield	Last ¼ 18th C	Very important, particularly his candlesticks, the best of which are the finest of the period
I·S	James Stamp	Early 4th ¼ 18th C	Good holloware, candlesticks, etc. (Note: similar to John Scofield's mark: they overlap for a short period, 1778-1780)
ISH / **ISH**	John Samuel Hunt ″ ″	Mid 19th C ″ ″	Major 19th C firm, originates with Paul Storr
JT	John Tuite	Mostly 2nd ¼ 18th C	Specialist salver maker
I·W RG	J Wakelin & Robert Garrard	Late 18th/very early 19th C	Important makers
IWS WE	J W Story & W Elliott	Early 19th C	Good makers
I·W WT	John Wakelin & William Taylor	Last ¼ 18th C	Important makers
IY	James Young	2nd ½ 18th C	Good, run-of-the-mill maker
IY OI	James Young & Orlando Jackson	2nd ½ 18th C	Good makers
JA	Joseph Angell	1st ½ 19th C	Very fine 19th C family of goldsmiths
J·A	″ ″	Mid 19th C	
JA IA	Joseph & John Angell	1st ½ 19th C	
J·A J·A	Joseph Angell sen & Joseph Angell jun	2nd ¼ 19th C	
JA JS	John Aldwinckle & James Slater	Late 19th C	Good makers
J A S H E	Joseph, Albert, Horace & Ethelbert Savory	Late 19th C	Large 19th C firm
JA TS	John Aldwinckle & Thomas Slater	Late 19th C	Good makers
JB	John Barbe	Mid 18th C	Good, run-of-the-mill maker

MARK	MAKER	PERIOD	COMMENTS
	Joseph Barbut	1st ¼ 18th C	Spoon maker
	Jes Barkentin (of Barkentin & Krall)	2nd ½ 19th C	Highly important work in 1860s for William Burgess
	James Beebe	Early 19th C	Spoon maker
	Carrington & Co	Late 19th/Early 20th C	Important retailers
	" "	" "	
	John Bodman Carrington (Carrington & Co)		
	James Barclay Hennell	Late 19th C	Good maker
	John Cafe	Mid 18th C	Specialist candlestick maker
	Jacques Cartier	20th C	Famous jeweller
	John Collard Vickery	20th C	Retailers
	John Denzilow	Last ¼ 18th C	Good, run-of-the-mill maker
	James Dixon & Sons - 20th C mark	20th C	Sheffield manufacturers
	John & William Deakin (James Deakin & Sons Ltd)	Late 19th/Early 20th C	Sheffield manufacturers
	John Emes	End 18th/Early 19th C	Wide range of run-of-the-mill work; prolific maker of tea and coffee sets
	" "	" "	
	John, Edward, Walter & John Barnard (Barnard & Sons Ltd)	2nd ½ 19th C	Major manufacturers
	James Garrard	Late 19th C	Important maker
	James Goodwin - post 1721 sterling mark	1st ¼ 18th C	Small mugs, peppers, etc.
	James Gould	Mid 18th C	Specialist candlestick maker
	" "	Late 1st/2nd ¼ 18th C	

MARK	MAKER	PERIOD	COMMENTS
	John Harvey	Mid 18th C	Found particularly on wine labels
	Joseph Heming	Late 19th/Early 20th C	Important retailer of silver and jewellery
	Joseph Heming & Co	Late 19th/Early 20th C	Important retailer of silver and jewellery
	John Lampfert	3rd ¼ 18th C	Specialist spoon maker. Often fine and interesting examples
	John Linnit	Early 19th C	Very good small work
	John Newton Mappin	Late 19th/Early 20th C	Very large Sheffield manufacturers
	"	"	
	"	"	
	"	"	
	"	"	
	John Newton Mappin & George Webb	"	
	John Payne	3rd ¼ 18th C	Good work
	John Pollock	Mid 18th C	Good, run-of-the-mill maker
	John Paul Cooper	20th C	Interesting and important maker
	Joseph Ridge (John Round & Son Ltd)	Late 19th/Early 20th C	Large Sheffield manufacturers
	John Round & Son Ltd	"	
	John le Sage	1st ½ 18th C	Important Huguenot goldsmith
	James Schruder	Mid 18th C	Very fine maker, who produced very interesting rococo
	John Schuppe	3rd ¼ 18th C	Specialist maker of cow creamers (much sought after)
	John Swift	Mid 18th C	Good tankards and other holloware

MARK	MAKER	PERIOD	COMMENTS

JS AS / J.S A S	Joseph & Albert Savory
	
	    " "
		Mid 19th C
		
		  " "
			Large 19th C firm

JSH	Joseph & Horace Savory	Late 19th C	Large 19th C firm
JT	John Tuite	Mostly 2nd ¼ 18th C	Specialist salver maker
JTH JHM	John Heath & John Middleton (of Hukin & Heath)	Late 19th/Early 20th C	Most important for their pieces designed by Dr C Dresser
J.V	Joshua Vander	Early 20th C	Important manufacturing silversmith
JV JH	John Vander & John Hedges (Tessiers)	Late 19th/Early 20th C	Important manufacturing silversmith

JW / JW	John James Whiting
	
	    " "
		Mid 19th C
		
		  " "
			Spoon maker

JW	James Wintle	2nd ¼ 19th C	Spoon maker
JW	John Wirgman	Mid 18th C	A fine maker
JW	John Wren	Late 18th C	Spoon maker

J.W.B / J.W.B.LD	J W Benson Ltd
	
	    " "
		Late 19th/Early 20th C
		
		  " "
			Important firm

JWD	James Dixon & Sons	Late 19th/Early 20th C	Large Sheffield manufacturer
JW FCW	James Wakely & Frank Wheeler	Late 19th/Early 20th C	Large manufacturer
JWH JTM	Hukin & Heath	Late 19th/Early 20th C	(It is this mark which is found on pieces designed for the firm by Dr C Dresser in the 1870s/80s)
KA / KA MU	Charles Frederick Kandler Chas Kandler & Jas Murray	Mid 18th C	Highly important, one of all-time greats Little is known of Murray
LA	Paul de Lamerie	1st ½ 18th C	Highly important, highly sought after, highly priced. Probably the most famous of all 18th C goldsmiths

MARK	MAKER	PERIOD	COMMENTS
	Jno Ladyman	Late 17th/Early 18th C	Specialist spoon maker. Do not confuse this mark with Paul de Lamerie!
	Geo Lambe	1st ¼ 18th C	Spoon maker
	John Laughton II	Late 17th/Early 18th C	Specialist maker of fine candlesticks
LAC	Lionel Alfred Crichton (Crichton Brothers)	20th C	Retailers of usually fine reproductions of early pieces
LC	Louisa Courtauld	3rd ¼ 18th C	Fine and interesting woman silversmith
LC GC	Louisa Courtauld & George Cowles	" "	Fine makers
LC SC	Louisa & Samuel Courtauld	Last ¼ 18th C	Fine makers
	Samuel Lea	1st ¼ 18th C	Good holloware
	Ralph Leeke	Early 18th C	Important English maker
LE	Timothy Ley	Late 17th/Early 18th C	Standard English tankards and mugs
LX	Louis Hamon	Mid 18th C	Very fine, difficult to find
F L★H B	Lewis Herne & Francis Butty	3rd ¼ 18th C	Good makers
F L★H B	" "	" "	
LI	Isaac Liger	1st ¼ 18th C	Fine Huguenot pieces sometimes engraved by Simon Gribelin, in which case, very important
LM	Lewis Mettayer - post 1720 sterling mark	1st ½ 18th C	Very important Huguenot
Lo	Nathaniel Lock	Late 17th/Early 18th C	Not the best of English work
	Mathew Lofthouse	Early 18th C	Mostly drinking vessels
Lo	Seth Lofthouse	1st ¼ 18th C	Competent English work
Lu	Wm Lukin	Early 18th C	Some very good pieces, mostly from George I period onwards
LY & CO	Liberty & Co	Late 19th/Early 20th C	Highly important Art Nouveau pieces designed by Archibald Knox

MARK	MAKER	PERIOD	COMMENTS
	Geo Manjoy	Late 17th/Early 18th C	Specialist maker of miniatures/toys. Very collectable
	" " (probably)	" "	
	Jacob Margas	1st ¼ 18th C	Good Huguenot
	Samuel Margas	Late 1st ¼/2nd ¼ 18th C	Good maker with a wide range
	Thos Mason	1st ½ 18th C	Good prolific maker, wide range
	Wm Mathew	Late 17th/Early 18th C	Good English work
	Moses Brent	Late 18th/Early 19th C	Prolific knife maker
	Mary Chawner	2nd ¼ 19th C	Spoon maker
	Mary Chawner & George W Adams	1840	Spoon makers
	Marmaduke Daintrey	Mid 18th C	Mostly a specialist spoon maker. Worked later in his life at Hartley Row in Hampshire
	" "	" "	
	Thomas Merry I (probably)	1st ¼ 18th C	Maker of fine candlesticks, tapersticks
	Lewis Mettayer	1st ½ 18th C	Important Huguenot work which may be linked with his brother-in-law, David Willaume, to whom he was also apprenticed
	Meshach Godwin - post 1722 sterling mark	Late 1st/2nd ¼ 18th C	Mostly run-of-the-mill peppers and other small pieces
	John Millington	1st ½ 18th C	Spoon maker
	Mathw Lofthouse - post 1720 sterling mark	Early 18th C	Mostly drinking vessels
	Mappin & Webb Ltd	Late 19th/Early 20th C	Very large manufacturers
	" " - 20th C mark	" "	
	Thos Morse	1st ¼ 18th C	Mostly good holloware
	Mary Pantin	2nd ¼ 18th C	Fine woman silversmith

MARK	MAKER	PERIOD	COMMENTS
	Mary Rood - post 1720 sterling mark	1st ½ 18th C	Salts
	Francis Nelme - post 1722 sterling mark, but used by his father before 1697	c.2nd ¼ 18th C	Important, but overshadowed by his father
	Bowles Nash	1st ½ 18th C	Mostly good holloware and salvers
	Nathaniel Appleton & Ann Smith	2nd ½ 18th C	Prolific makers of cream jugs
	Nayler Brothers	20th C	Manufacturing silversmiths
	Nicholas Clausen - post 1720 sterling mark	1st ¼ 18th C	Important and interesting maker whose work is difficult to find
	Nich Dumee	Last ¼ 18th C	Good, run-of-the-mill maker
	Anthony Nelme	Late 17th/Early 18th C	Probably the most important English goldsmith of the period
	Nathaniel Gulliver	2nd ¼ 18th C	Good holloware, particularly coffee pots
	Nicholas Sprimont	Mid 18th C	Extremely important, extremely rare, extremely valuable work
	Orlando Jackson	2nd ½ 18th C	Good maker
	" "	" "	
	Ollivant & Botsford	Late 19th/Early 20th C	Manchester retailers
	Chas Overing	Late 17th/Early 18th C	Good large pieces
	Benjamin Pyne - pre-1679 & post 1720 sterling mark	Late 17th/Early 18th C	Important English goldsmith of the period
	Peter Archambo I - post 1720 sterling mark	1st ½ 18th C	Important Huguenot
	" "	" "	
	Simon Pantin	Early 18th C	Very good Huguenot
	" "	" "	
	Wm Paradise	1st ½ 18th C	Mostly good mugs and tankards

MARK	MAKER	PERIOD	COMMENTS
	Thomas Parr I	Late 17th/Early 18th C	Mostly good English holloware
	Humph Payne	1st ½ 18th C	Good English maker, quite prolific
	" "	" "	
	Peter Archambo II & Peter Meure	3rd ¼ 18th C	Fine makers
	Peter & Ann Bateman	Late 18th C	Prolific, run-of-the-mill manufacturers
	Peter, Ann & William Bateman	Early 19th C	Prolific, general run-of-the-mill work
	Peter & Jonathan Bateman	1790	Much sought by Bateman collectors; mark used for less than six months
	Peter & William Bateman	Early 19th C	Prolific, run-of-the-mill makers
	Paul Callard	3rd ¼ 18th C	Mostly spoons
	Paul Crespin	Mid 18th C	Highly important and serious rival to Paul de Lamerie, certainly his equal
	" "	" "	
	" " - post 1720 sterling mark	" "	
	William Petley	1st ¼ 18th C	Spoon maker
	Phillips Garden	Mid 18th C	Fine technician; acquired and used Paul de Lamerie's casting patterns after 1752 (these pieces are much sought after)
	" "	" "	
	" "	" "	
	" "	" "	
	Pierre Gillois	2nd ½ 18th C	Specialist caddy maker
	Paul Hanet - post 1721 sterling mark	1st/2nd ¼ 18th C	Huguenot spoon maker
	Pézé Pilleau	Late 1st/2nd ¼ 18th C	Fine Huguenot, who also made false teeth!

MARK	MAKER	PERIOD	COMMENTS
	Paul de Lamerie " " - post 1733 sterling mark	1st ½ 18th C " "	Highly important, highly sought after, highly priced; probably the most famous of all 18th C goldsmiths
	Pierre Platel	Late 17th/Early 18th C	Extremely important Master of Paul de Lamerie
	Pézé Pilleau " " - post 1720 sterling mark	Late 1st/2nd ¼ 18th C " "	Fine Huguenot, who also made false teeth!
	Peter Podie	Last ¼ 18th C	Good maker
	Philip Rainaud - post 1720 sterling mark	1st ¼ 18th C	Very fine Huguenot work is rare. (Rainaud and Paul de Lamerie were the only apprentices of Pierre Platel)
	Philip Roker II " "	2nd ¼ 18th C " "	Specialist spoon maker
	Philip Roker III	Last ¼ 18th C	Spoon maker
	Philip Rollos II - post 1720 sterling mark	Late 17th/Early 18th C	Important Huguenot
	Philip Rundell	Early 19th C	Very important maker
	Paul Storr " "	Late 18th/1st ½ 19th C " "	Highly important, highly priced (most important work c.1807-20 when with Rundell, Bridge & Rundell; later work is less sought after)
	Benjamin Pyne " "	Late 17th/Early 18th C " "	Important English goldsmith of the period
	Roberts & Belk Ltd	Late 19th/Early 20th C	Sheffield manufacturers
	Alex Roode	Late 17th/Early 18th C	Salts & other plate
	Robert Abercromby " "	2nd ¼ 18th C " "	Specialist in good salvers

MARK	MAKER	PERIOD	COMMENTS
RA	Philip Rainaud	1st ¼ 18th C	Very fine Huguenot work is rare (Rainaud and Paul de Lamerie were the only apprentices of Pierre Platel)
GRYH	Robert Abercromby & George Hindmarsh	2nd ¼ 18th C	Specialist salver makers
RB	Richard Bayley	1st ½ 18th C	Prolific maker of good holloware
RB&R	Rundell, Bridge & Rundell	1st ¼ 19th C	Highly important makers
RC	Richard Crossley	Late 18th C	Spoon maker
RC DS RS	Richard Carter, Daniel Smith, Robert Sharp	Last ¼ 18th C	Important makers
RC GS	Richard Crossley & George Smith	Early 19th C	Spoon makers
RE EB	Rebecca Emes & Edward Barnard	Early 19th C	Very large output of good silver, many tea and coffee sets
R·E W·E	Rebecca & William Emes	1808	Mark only used for 3½ months, good work
RFF	Robert Frederick Fox	Early 20th C	Last member of this important family of goldsmiths
RG	Robert Garrard I	Early 19th C	Important maker
RG	Robert Garrard II	Early/Mid 19th C	
RG	" "	Mid 19th C	
RS	" "	" "	
RG	Richard Gosling	Mid 18th C	Specialist spoon maker
RGC	Richard Gurney & Co	Mid 18th C	Usually good, run-of-the-mill holloware
T RG C	Richard Gurney & Thomas Cook	" "	
R·H	Robert Hennell II	1st ⅓ 19th C	Good maker

MARK	MAKER	PERIOD	COMMENTS
RH	Robert Hennell	Last ¼ 18th C	Good, general work; some particularly fine pierced coasters
RH	" "	Mid 19th C	Very fine work
RH DH	Robert & David Hennell	Late 18th/Early 19th C	Good, general work
RH DH SH	Robert, David & Samuel Hennell	Early 19th C	Good makers
RH SH	Robert & Samuel Hennell	Early 19th C	Good makers
RI	Isaac Ribouleau	2nd ¼ 18th C	Fine Huguenot, but difficult to find
RI IS	Robert Jones & John Scofield	1776-1778	First work of the important maker John Scofield
RM	Robert Makepeace	Late 18th C	Good maker
RM EH / RM EH	Martin, Hall & Co Ltd	2nd ½ 19th/Early 20th C	Large Sheffield manufacturers
	" "	" "	
RM RC	Robert Makepeace & Richard Carter	Last ¼ 18th C	Fine makers
RM TM	Robert & Thomas Makepeace	Late 18th C	Good makers
RN&CR	Omar Ramsden & Alwyn Carr	Late 19th/Early 20th C	The most important work of Ramsden is during this partnership
RO	Philip Roker II	c.2nd ¼ 18th C	Spoon maker
RO	Philip Rollos II	Early 18th C	Important Huguenot
Ro	Philip Rollos	Late 17th/Early 18th C	Important Huguenot
RO	James Rood	1st ¼ 18th C	Specialist salt maker
RO	Mary Rood	1st ½ 18th C	Salts
R‡P	R Peaston	3rd ¼ 18th C	Often found on casters (run-of-the-mill)

MARK	MAKER	PERIOD	COMMENTS
R·R	Robert Rew	3rd ¼ 18th C	Salver maker
RR R·R	Richard Rugg " "	3rd ¼ 18th C " "	Salver maker. Both Rew and Rugg worked at the same time and specialised in making salvers (Rew's is the largest of the marks)
R·R·A·H·I·M·H	Hunt & Roskell - late 19th C mark	Late 19th/Early 20th C	Major 19th C firm, originates with Paul Storr
RS	Robert Sharp	Late 18th C	Important maker
RS R·S	Richard Sibley " "	1st ½ 19th C " "	A very fine goldsmith
RU	John Ruslen	Late 17th/Early 18th C	One of the best English makers of the period
SA	Stephen Adams	2nd ½ 18th C	Spoon maker
SA	Stephen Adams, jun	Early 19th C	Spoon maker
SA	John Hugh le Sage	1st ½ 18th C	Important Huguenot gold-smith
S B S·B	Susanna Barker " "	Last ¼ 18th C " "	Usually small pieces
S·C S·C	Samuel Courtauld " "	Mid 18th C " "	Fine Huguenot work
SC	Wm Scarlett	Late 17th/Early 18th C	Specialist spoon maker - beware of forgeries
S·C I·C	Sebastian & James Crespell	3rd ¼ 18th C	Prolific makers of plates and dishes
Se	Jas Seabrook	1st ¼ 18th C	Mostly good tapersticks
SG JG	Sebastian Harry Garrard - 20th C mark " "	Late 19th/Early 20th C 20th C	Important maker
SG	Samuel Godbehere	Last ¼ 18th C	Good, run-of-the-mill maker

MARK	MAKER	PERIOD	COMMENTS
	Samuel Godbehere & Edward Wigan	Last ¼ 18th C	Good, general makers of usually small pieces, spoons, cream jugs, etc.
	Samuel Godbehere, Edward Wigan & James Boult	" "	
	Samuel Herbert	Mid 18th C	Mostly pierced work, baskets, etc.
	Sarah Holaday - post 1725 sterling mark	Late 1st ¼/2nd ¼ 18th C	This mark is often confused with Alice Sheene's, which is earlier and always Britannia standard. Good woman silversmith.
	Solomon Hougham	Late 18th/Early 19th C	Run-of-the-mill maker
	Alice Sheene	1st ¼ 18th C	Good woman silversmith (do not confuse this mark with Sarah Holaday's, which is later (1725 on))
	Solomon Hougham, Solomon Royes & John East Dix	Early 19th C	Good, run-of-the-mill work
	Herbert & Co	Mid 18th C	Mostly pierced work, baskets, etc.
	S. Herbert & Co	" "	
	Francis Singleton	Late 17th/Early 18th C	Competent English work
	Simon Jouet	2nd ¼ 18th C	Fine maker
	" "	" "	
	Solomon Joel Phillips	20th C	Mark usually found on very fine copies of early pieces
	Simon le Sage	3rd ¼ 18th C	Very fine Huguenot goldsmith
	" "	" "	
	Gabriel Sleath	1st ½ 18th C	Prolific, good English work
	" "	" "	
	Saml Margas - post 1720 sterling mark	Late 1st ¼/2nd ¼ 18th C	Good maker with a wide range

MARK	MAKER	PERIOD	COMMENTS
SM	S Mordan & Co Ltd	Late 19th/Early 20th C	Very collectable small pieces; vast numbers of pencils
SM&Co	" "	" "	
SM &Co	" "	" "	
SP	Simon Pantin - post 1720 sterling mark	Early 18th C	Very good Huguenot
S·P	Simon Pantin II	2nd ¼ 18th C	Good Huguenot goldsmith
Sp	Thos Spackman	Early 18th C	Spoons
S·P	Wm Spackman	1st ¼ 18th C	Good, run-of-the-mill, general work
S·R C·B	Roberts & Belk Ltd - late 19th C mark	Late 19th/Early 20th C	Sheffield manufacturers
S.S	Stephen Smith	2nd ½ 19th C	Very fine silversmith
S.S.	" "	" "	
S.S W·N	Stephen Smith & William Nicholson	Mid 19th C	Very fine silversmiths
S.S W.N	" "	" "	
St	Ambrose Stevenson	1st ¼ 18th C	Wide range
St	Saml Taylor	Mid 18th C	Good holloware
SW	Samuel Welder	Late 1st ¼/2nd ¼ 18th C	Specialist and prolific caster maker
sw	" " - post 1720 sterling mark	1st ¼ 18th C	
SW	Samuel Wintle	Last ¼ 18th C	Spoon maker (many sugar tongs)
SW	Samuel Wood	Mid 18th C	Specialist and prolific caster maker
S·W	" "	" "	
S·W	" "	" "	

MARK	MAKER	PERIOD	COMMENTS
	Richard Syng	Late 17th/Early 18th C	Competent, but not great English holloware
	Ann Tanqueray	2nd ¼ 18th C	Probably the greatest of all women silversmiths
	David Tanqueray	1st ¼ 18th C	Very fine Huguenot work associated with his father-in-law, David Willaume
	Thomas Bamford	c.2nd ¼ 18th C	Prolific maker of good, run-of-the-mill casters
	Thomas Bradbury & Sons	Late 19th/Early 20th C	Sheffield manufacturers
	" "	" "	
	" "	" "	
	Robert Timbrell & Joseph Bell	1st ¼ 18th C	Good holloware
	Thomas Bumfriss & Orlando Jackson	2nd ½ 18th C	Good makers
	Thomas Chawner	2nd ½ 18th C	Spoon maker
	T Cox Savory	2nd ¼ 19th C	Large 19th C firm
	Thomas & William Chawner	3rd ¼ 18th C	Specialist and very fine flatware makers
	" "	" "	
	" "	" "	
	" "	" "	
	Thomas Daniel	Last ¼ 18th C	Good, run-of-the-mill maker
	" "	" "	
	Thomas Dealtry	2nd ½ 18th C	Flatware and knife handles
	Thomas Daniel & John Wall	Last ¼ 18th C	Good, run-of-the-mill makers
	Thomas Tearle	1st ½ 18th C	Good, run-of-the-mill maker

MARK	MAKER	PERIOD	COMMENTS
	Thomas Farren	1st ½ 18th C	Very fine maker
	" " - post 1720 sterling mark	" "	
	Thos Folkingham - post 1720 sterling mark	1st ¼ 18th C	Wide range of fine silver
	Thomas Gilpin	Mid 18th C	A very fine goldsmith
	Thomas Heming	2nd ½ 18th C	Important maker; Royal goldsmith
	" "	" "	
	" "	" "	
	Thomas & George Hayter	1st ½ 19th C	Mostly spoon makers
	Thomas Hannam & John Crouch	2nd ½ 18th C	Very good makers
	Thomas Hannam & John Crouch (or Carter)	" "	Fine salvers
	Robert Timbrell	Late 17th/Early 18th C	Good English work
	Timothy Ley - pre 1697 and post 1720 sterling mark	Late 17th/Early 18th C	Standard English tankards and mugs
	Thomas Morley	Last ¼ 18th C	Small pieces
	Thomas Northcote	Late 18th C	Spoon maker
	Thomas Northcote & George Bourne	Late 18th/Early 19th C	Good, general work; usually smaller pieces
	Thomas Pitts	2nd ½ 18th C	Specialist in pierced work, epergnes, baskets, etc.
	Thomas Phipps & Edward Robinson	Last ¼ 18th C	Usually very fine boxes, etc., but can be found on large pieces
	" "	Late 18th/Early 19th C	
	Thomas Phipps, Edward Robinson & James Phipps	" "	

MARK	MAKER	PERIOD	COMMENTS
TS WS HB	Thomas, Walter & Henry Holland - late 19th C mark	Late 19th/Early 20th C	Important manufacturers
TT	Thomas Tearle - post 1720 sterling mark	1st ½ 18th C	Good run-of-the-mill maker
TW	Thomas Wallis	Last ¼ 18th C	Spoon maker
TW	" "	Late 18th/Early 19th C	
TW	Thomas Whipham	Mid 18th C	Prolific maker of good holloware, particularly coffee pots, teapots, tankards and mugs
TW	" "	" "	
TW	" "	" "	
CTW	Thomas Whipham & Charles Wright	2nd ½ 18th C	Prolific makers of holloware, particularly coffee pots, teapots, tankards and mugs
V·I	Edward Vincent	1st ½ 18th C	Very fine English craftsman, who could be naughty; he was into duty dodging after 1720 in a big way: be careful
W&H	Walker & Hall - 20th C mark	20th C	Large Sheffield manufacturer
&WW	Wakely & Wheeler - 20th C mark	20th C	Large manufacturers and silversmiths
WA	William Abdy	Last ¼ 18th C	Good, run-of-the-mill maker
WA	Joseph Ward	Late 17th/Early 18th C	Very good English work
WA	Sam Wastell	Early 18th C	Good English work
W·A	" "	" "	
Wa	Benjamin Watts	Late 17th/Early 18th C	Mostly spoons
W·B	William Bateman	1st ½ 19th C	Very good (best of the Batemans)
W·B	Walter Brind	2nd ½ 18th C	Prolific maker of good holloware
WB	" "	" "	
WB	William Burwash	Early 19th C	Good maker

MARK	MAKER	PERIOD	COMMENTS
WB DB	William Bateman & Daniel Ball	2nd ¼ 19th C	Prolific, general run-of-the-mill work
 WB DB	" "	" "	
 WBJ	Walter & John Barnard	Late 19th C	Major manufacturers
W·B R·S	William Burwash & Richard Sibley	1st ¼ 19th C	Very good makers
 WC	William Cafe	3rd ¼ 18th C	Specialist candlestick maker
 WC	William Chawner	1st ¼ 19th C	Prolific spoon maker
 W.C	William Comyns & Sons Ltd	2nd ½ 19th/Early 20th C	Large manufacturer
 WC	" "	" "	
WC	William Cripps	Mid 18th C	Very fine work
WC	" "	" "	
WD	Wm Darker - post 1720 sterling mark	1st ½ 18th C	Good general maker, quite prolific
WE	William Eaton	Late 1st ¼/2nd ¼ 19th C	Spoon maker
 WE	" "	" "	
 WE	William Eley II	2nd ¼ 19th C	Spoon maker
 WE	Robert Eley	Late 18th/Early 19th C	Spoon maker
 We	Saml Welder	1st ¼ 18th C	Prolific maker of casters
 WE CE HE	William, Charles & Henry Eley	c.1824	Spoon makers
WE WF	William Eley & William Fearn	Late 18th/Early 19th C	Prolific spoon makers
 WE WF WC	William Eley, William Fearn & William Chawner	1st ¼ 19th C	Prolific spoon makers
 WF	William Fearn	2nd ½ 18th C	Prolific spoon maker

MARK	MAKER	PERIOD	COMMENTS
WF	William Fountain	Late 18th/Early 19th C	Good, general work
WF DP	William Fountain & Daniel Pontifex	Late 18th C	Good makers
WF PS	William Frisbee & Paul Storr	1792-3	First work of the highly important Paul Storr
WG	William Gould	Mid 18th C	Specialist candlestick maker
WG	" "	" "	
WG	" "	" "	
WG	William Grundy	Mid 18th C	Good holloware maker
WG	" "	" "	
WG	" "	" "	
WG	" "	" "	
WG	" "	" "	
E WG F	William Grundy & Edward Fernell	Mid 18th C	Good, run-of-the-mill makers
WG JL	William Gibson & John Langman	Late 19th/Early 20th C	Retail jewellers and silversmiths
W.G J.L	" "	" "	
WH	William Holmes	Last ¼ 18th C	Good maker
S&L	William Hutton & Sons Ltd	2nd ½ 19th/Early 20th C	Large Sheffield manufacturers
WH ND	William Holmes & Nich Dumee	Last ¼ 18th C	Good makers
W.H.S	Searle & Co	20th C	Retailers
WI	George Wickes	Mostly 2nd ¼ 18th C	Very important English goldsmith
WI	Starling Wilford	2nd ¼ 18th C	Mostly casters
WI	David Willaume	Late 17th/Early 18th C	Very important Huguenot
WI	David Willaume II	2nd ¼ 18th C	Important Huguenot

MARK	MAKER	PERIOD	COMMENTS
WK	William Kidney	Mid 18th C	A fine goldsmith, often underrated
WK	" "	" "	
WBJ MBS	Edward Barnard & Sons Ltd	20th C	Major manufacturers
WP	Wm Peaston	Mid 18th C	Specialist salver maker
W·P	William Plummer	3rd ¼ 18th C	Specialist in pierced work
WP	William Pitts	Last ¼ 18th C	Specialist in pierced work, epergnes, baskets, etc.
W·P I·P	William Pitts & Joseph Preedy	End 18th C	Pierced work, baskets, epergnes, etc.
W·P J·P	W & J Priest	Late 18th C	Standard work
W·R&H·	Walker & Hall - late 19th C mark	Late 19th/Early 20th C	Large Sheffield manufacturers
WRS	W R Smily	Mid 19th C	Spoon maker
W·S	William Shaw	3rd ¼ 18th C	Good holloware maker
WS	William Spackman - post 1720 sterling mark	1st ¼ 18th C	Good run-of-the-mill general work
W·S	William Sumner	Early 19th C	Spoon maker
WS CS	Walter & Charles Sissons	Late 19th C	Sheffield manufacturers
WS GS	William & George Sissons	3rd ¼ 19th C	
WS RC	William Sumner & Richard Crossley	Last ¼ 18th C	Good, run-of-the-mill makers
W·S P	William Shaw & William Priest	3rd ¼ 18th C	Makers of good holloware
W·T	Walter Thornhill (Thornhill & Co)	19th C	Retailer of very fine pieces
WT RA	William Theobalds & Robert Atkinson	2nd ¼ 19th C	Mostly fine flatware
WV	William Vincent	Last ¼ 18th C	Run-of-the-mill teapots, etc.

Birmingham

Cycles of Hallmarks

CYCLE I

	LION PASSANT	ANCHOR	DATE LETTER	DUTY MARK
1773-74	[lion passant]	[anchor]	A	
1774-75	"	"	B	
1775-76	"	"	C	
1776-77	"	"	D	
1777-78	"	"	E	
1778-79	"	"	F	
1779-80	"	"	G	
1780-81	"	"	H	
1781-82	"	"	I	
1782-83	"	"	K	
1783-84	"	"	L	
Up to 30 Nov. 1784	"	"	M	
From 1 Dec. 1784-July 1785	"	"	"	[duty mark]
1785-86	"	"	N	"
1786-87	"	"	O	[duty mark]
1787-88	"	"	P	"
1788-89	"	"	Q	"
1789-90	"	"	R	"
1790-91	"	"	S	"
1791-92	"	"	T	"
1792-93	"	"	U	"
1793-94	"	"	V	"
1794-95	"	"	W	"
1795-96	"	"	X	"
1796-97	"	"	Y	"
1797	"	"	Z	"
1797-98*	"	"	"	[two duty marks]
	"	"	"	[duty mark]

CYCLE II

	LION PASSANT	ANCHOR	DATE LETTER	DUTY MARK
1798-99	[lion passant]	[anchor]	a	[duty mark]
1799-1800	"	"	b	"
1800-1 ‡	"	"	c	"
1801-2	"	"	d	"
1802-3	"	"	e	"
1803-4	"	"	f	"
1804-5	"	"	g	"
1805-6	"	"	h	"
1806-7	"	"	i	"
1807-8	"	"	j	"
1808-9	"	"	k	"
1809-10	"	"	l	[duty mark]
1810-11	"	"	m	"
1811-12	"	"	n	"
1812-13	"	"	o	[duty mark]
1813-14	"	"	p	"
1814-15	"	"	q	"
1815-16	"	"	r	"
1816-17	"	"	s	"
1817-18	"	"	t	"
1818-19	"	"	u	"
1819-20	"	"	v	"
GEO.IV 1820-21	"	"	w	"
1821-22	"	"	x	"
1822-23	"	"	y	"
1823-24	"	"	z	"

* Double duty.

‡ On plate of 1801 to 1811 the King's head mark is frequently found in a stamp of oval shape, and on plate of 1812 to 1825 it is sometimes in a foliated stamp as shown at 1797-98 and 1809-10.

CYCLE III

	LION PASSANT	ANCHOR	DATE LETTER	DUTY MARK
1824-25			A	
1825-26	"	"	B	"
1826-27	"	"	C	
1827-28	"	"	D	"
1828-29	"	"	E	"
1829-30	"	"	F	
WM.IV 1830-31	"	"	G	"
1831-32	"	"	H	
1832-33	"	"	I	"
1833-34	"	"	K	"
1834-35	"	"	L	
1835-36	"	"	M	"
1836-37	"	"	N	"
VICT. 1837-38	"	"	O	"
1838-39*	"	"	P	
1839-40	"	"	Q	"
1840-41	"	"	R	"
1841-42	"	"	S	"
1842-43	"	"	T	"
1843-44	"	"	U	"
1844-45	"	"	V	"
1845-46	"	"	W	"
1846-47	"	"	X	"
1847-48	"	"	Y	"
1848-49	"	"	Z	"

CYCLE IV

	LION PASSANT	ANCHOR	DATE LETTER	DUTY MARK
1849-50			A	
1850-51	"	"	B	"
1851-52	"	"	C	"
1852-53	"	"	D	"
1853-54	"	"	E	"
1854-55	"	"	F	"
1855-56	"	"	G	"
1856-57	"	"	H	"
1857-58	"	"	I	"
1858-59	"	"	J	"
1859-60	"	"	K	"
1860-61	"	"	L	"
1861-62	"	"	M	"
1862-63	"	"	N	"
1863-64	"	"	O	"
1864-65	"	"	P	"
1865-66	"	"	Q	"
1866-67 †	"	"	R	"
1867-68	"	"	S	"
1868-69	"	"	T	"
1869-70	"	"	U	"
1870-71	"	"	V	"
1871-72	"	"	W	"
1872-73	"	"	X	"
1873-74	"	"	Y	"
1874-75	"	"	Z	"

* On plate of the early part of 1838-39 the head of King William is sometimes found stamped, although Queen Victoria succeeded to the throne in 1837.

† F was struck on imported wares in addition to the marks shown from 1867-1904.

CYCLE V

	LION PASSANT	ANCHOR	DATE LETTER	DUTY MARK
1875-76	🦁	⚓	ⓐ	👑
1876-77	"	"	ⓑ	"
1877-78	"	"	ⓒ	"
1878-79	"	"	ⓓ	"
1879-80	"	"	ⓔ	"
1880-81	"	"	ⓕ	"
1881-82	"	"	ⓖ	"
1882-83	"	"	ⓗ	"
1883-84	"	"	ⓘ	"
1884-85	"	"	ⓚ	"
1885-86	"	"	ⓛ	"
1886-87	"	"	ⓜ	"
1887-88	"	"	ⓝ	"
1888-89	"	"	ⓞ	"
Up to 1 May 1890	"	"	ⓟ	"
2 May to July 1890	"	"	"	
1890-91	"	"	ⓠ	
1891-92	"	"	ⓡ	
1892-93	"	"	ⓢ	
1893-94	"	"	ⓣ	
1894-95	"	"	ⓤ	
1895-96	"	"	ⓥ	
1896-97	"	"	ⓦ	
1897-98	"	"	ⓧ	
1898-99	"	"	ⓨ	
1899-1900	"	"	ⓩ	

CYCLE VI

	ANCHOR	LION PASSANT	DATE LETTER
1900-1	⚓	🦁	ⓐ
EDW.VII 1901-2	"	"	ⓑ
1902-3	"	"	ⓒ
1903-4	"	"	ⓓ
1904-5	"	"	ⓔ
1905-6	"	"	ⓕ
1906-7	"	"	ⓖ
1907-8	"	"	ⓗ
1908-9	"	"	ⓘ
1909-10	"	"	ⓚ
GEO.V 1910-11	"	"	ⓛ
1911-12	"	"	ⓜ
1912-13	"	"	ⓝ
1913-14	"	"	ⓞ
1914-15	"	"	ⓟ
1915-16	"	"	ⓠ
1916-17	"	"	ⓡ
1917-18	"	"	ⓢ
1918-19	"	"	ⓣ
1919-20	"	"	ⓤ
1920-21	"	"	ⓥ
1921-22	"	"	ⓦ
1922-23	"	"	ⓧ
1923-24	"	"	ⓨ
1924-25	"	"	ⓩ

CYCLE VII

	ANCHOR	LION PASSANT	DATE LETTER
1925-26	⚓	🦁	A
1926-27	"	"	B
1927-28	"	"	C
1928-29	"	"	D
1929-30	"	"	E
1930-31	"	"	F
1931-32	"	"	G
1932-33	"	"	H
1933-34	"	"	J
1934-35*	"	"	K
1935-36*	"	"	L
EDW.VIII 1936-37	"	"	M
GEO.VI 1937-38	"	"	N
1938-39	"	"	O
1939-40	"	"	P
1940-41	"	"	Q
1941-42	"	"	R
1942-43	"	"	S
1943-44	"	"	T
1944-45	"	"	U
1945-46	"	"	V
1946-47	"	"	W
1947-48	"	"	X
1948-49	"	"	Y
1949-50	"	"	Z

CYCLE VIII

	ANCHOR	LION PASSANT	DATE LETTER
1950-51	⚓	🦁	A
1951-52	"	"	B
ELIZ.II 1952-53 ǂ	"	"	C
1953-54 ǂ	"	"	D
1954-55	"	"	E
1955-56	"	"	F
1956-57	"	"	G
1957-58	"	"	H
1958-59	"	"	J
1959-60	"	"	K
1960-61	"	"	L
1961-62	"	"	M
1962-63	"	"	N
1963-64	"	"	O
1964-65	"	"	P
1965-66	"	"	Q
1966-67	"	"	R
1967-68	"	"	S
1968-69	"	"	T
1969-70	"	"	U
1970-71	"	"	V
1971-72	"	"	W
1972-73	"	"	X
1973-74	⚓	🦁	Y
Up to 31 Dec.1974	⚓	🦁	Z

  There was an optional Silver Jubilee mark for these two years.

 There was an optional Coronation mark for these years.

CYCLE IX

	ANCHOR	LION PASSANT	DATE LETTER
1975	⚓	🦁	𝓐
1976	"	"	𝓑
1977*	"	"	𝓒
1978	"	"	𝓓
1979	"	"	𝓔
1980	"	"	𝓕
1981	"	"	𝓖
1982	"	"	𝓗
1983	"	"	𝓙
1984	"	"	𝓚
1985	"	"	𝓛
1986	"	"	𝓜
1987	"	"	𝓝
1988	"	"	𝓞
1989	"	"	𝓟
1990	"	"	𝓠
1991	"	"	𝓡

*   There is an optional Silver Jubilee mark for this year.

PLATINUM 1975

	ANCHOR	PLATINUM MARK	DATE LETTER
Date as Above	⚓	⬠	𝓐

GOLD MARKS

Since 1824, gold has been assayed at Birmingham in the same way as at London with the obvious difference of the anchor replacing the leopard's head.

As an example, the range of Birmingham gold marks for 1920-21 is given in the table on the right.

22ct.	👑	22	⚓	V
18ct	"	18	"	".
15ct.	15 ·625		"	"
12ct.	12 ·5		"	"
9ct.	9 375		"	"

IMPORT MARKS FROM 1904 ON

1904-32

IMPORTED GOLD				IMPORTED SILVER			
22ct.	△	·916	+ Date letter & sponsor's mark	Britannia	△	·9584	+ Date letter & sponsor's mark
20ct.	"	·833	"	Sterling	"	·925	"
18ct.	"	·75	"				
15ct.	"	·625	"				
12ct.	"	·5	"				
9ct.	"	·375	"				

1932-74*

GOLD				SILVER
22ct.	△	·916	+ Date letter & sponsor's mark	(As 1904-32)
18ct.	"	·750	"	
14ct.	"	·585	"	
9ct.	"	·375	"	

From 1975 on

Platinum	△	950	+ Date letter & sponsor's mark
Gold 22ct.	△	916	"
18ct.	"	750	"
14ct.	"	585	"
9ct.	"	375	"
Silver Britannia	△	925	"
Sterling	"	958	"

* In 1932 and from then on 14ct. replaced 15ct. and 12ct.

CONVENTION MARKS (Birmingham) 1976 on

PRECIOUS METAL	ASSAY OFFICE MARK	COMMON CONTROL MARK	FINENESS MARK
Platinum			950
Gold 18ct.	"		750
14ct.	"		585
9ct.	"		375
Sterling			925

Convention marking on imported wares

PRECIOUS METAL	ASSAY OFFICE MARK	COMMON CONTROL MARK	FINENESS MARK
Platinum			950
Gold 18ct.			750
14ct.	"		585
9ct.	"		375
Silver (Sterling)			925

MARK	MAKER	PERIOD	COMMENTS
	A & J Zimmerman Ltd	20th C	Manufacturer
	" "	" "	
	Adie Brothers	20th C	Large manufacturers
	Alexander Clark & Co	20th C	Manufacturers
	" "	" "	
	A E Jones	20th C	Manufacturers. Their Art Nouveau is collected although not top flight. More recently pieces designed by Eric Clements for the firm are very interesting
	Bernard Cuzner	1st ½ 20th C	Interesting work
	Barker Ellis Silver Co	2nd ½ 20th C	Manufacturers
	Birmingham Guild of Handicraft	End 19th/Early 20th C	Interesting Arts and Crafts
	" "	" "	
	Cocks & Bettridge	Early 19th C	Maker of boxes, vinaigrettes, caddy spoons, etc.
	Cyril Shiner	20th C	Particularly interesting Art Deco
	Charles Thomas	2nd ½ 20th C	Interesting Art Deco
	Deakin & Francis Ltd	20th C	Manufacturers
	Deakin & Harrison	1st ½ 20th C	Manufacturers
	" "	" "	
	" "	" "	
	Deykin & Son	End 19th/Early 20th C	Manufacturers

MARK	MAKER	PERIOD	COMMENTS
	Elkington & Co Ltd	19th C	Quality is always superb. Designs vary from run-of-the-mill commercial to extremely important to people like Morel-Ladueil and Dr C Dresser
	" "	Mid 19th C	
	" "	" "	Important 19th C firm with very wide range
	" "	19th C	
	" "	Late 19th C	
	" "	20th C	
	Elkington Mason & Co	19th C	
ES	Edward Smith	Mid 19th C	Boxes, etc.
FC	Francis Clark	Mid 19th C	Small work
	Nathan & Hayes	End 19th/Early 20th C	Manufacturers
GU	George Unite	Late 19th/Early 20th C	Wide range of small pieces
GW	Gervase Wheeler	Mid 19th C	Boxes, etc.
H&H	Hukin & Heath Ltd	Late 19th/Early 20th C	Most important for pieces by them designed by Dr C Dresser (late 1870s and 1880s)
H&H	" "	" "	
	" "	Early 20th C	
H&H	" "	2nd ¼ 20th C	
H&T	Hilliard & Thomason	2nd ½ 19th C	Card cases, caddy spoons, etc.
HM	H. Matthews	Late 19th/Early 20th C	Wide range
JB	John Bettridge	Early 19th C	Boxes, etc.
JS	John Shaw	Late 18th/Early 19th C	Boxes, vinaigrettes
JT	Joseph Taylor	Late 18th/Early 19th C	Prolific maker of small pieces

MARK	MAKER	PERIOD	COMMENTS
JB	Joseph Bettridge	2nd ¼ 19th C	Small work
JB	" "	" "	
J.B.C &S	J B Chatterley & Sons	End 19th/Early 20th C	Manufacturers
JBC &S L°	" "	" "	
J.B.C B	" "	" "	
J H.&C°	John Hardman & Co	Mid 19th/Early 20th C	Important Gothic revival pieces designed by A W N Pugin
JL	John Lawrence & Co	Mid 19th/Early 20th C	Small work
JTH JHM	Heath & Middleton	Late 19th C	Most important for pieces designed for them by Dr C Dresser (late 1870s and 1880s)
JW	Joseph Willmore	1st ½ 19th C	Prolific maker of boxes, vinaigrettes, caddy spoons, etc.
JW	" "	" "	
L&C	Lea & Clark	Early 19th C	Small work
L&C	W. Lea & Co	Early 19th C	Boxes, vinaigrettes, etc.
L&C°	Ledsam & Vale	Early 19th C	Boxes, etc.
L&C°	Liberty & Co	End 19th C/20th C	Important Art Nouveau
LS&C°	L. Smith & Co	20th C	Manufacturer
LV&W	Ledsam, Vale & Wheeler	2nd ¼ 19th C	Boxes
MB	Matthew Boulton	Late 18th/Early 19th C	Very important maker; wide range
MB IF	Matthew Boulton & John Fothergill	Late 18th C	
M B I F	" "	" "	
ML	Matthew Linwood	Late 18th/Early 19th C	Boxes, vinaigrettes, caddy spoons, etc.
ML	" "	" "	
ML	" "	" "	

MARK	MAKER	PERIOD	COMMENTS
N&H	Nathan & Hayes	Late 19th/Early 20th C	Wide range
NM	Nathaniel Mills	Mid 19th C	Famous maker of fine boxes, vinaigrettes, etc.
R W	Robert Welch	2nd ½ 20th C	Important modern designer
R W	" "	" "	
RW	" "	" "	
RW	" "	" "	
SGM	Stanley Morris	Mid/2nd ½ 20th C	Designer/craftsman; interesting work
SP	Samuel Pemberton	Late 18th/Early 19th C	Prolific maker of boxes, vinaigrettes, caddy spoons, etc.
S P	" "	" "	
SP	" "	" "	
SP	" "	" "	
S²H⁺ & L⁰	W Hutton & Sons Ltd	20th C	Manufacturer
SW	Silver Workshop	2nd ½ 20th C	Interesting designs
T&P	Taylor & Perry	2nd ¼ 19th C	Boxes, card cases, caddy spoons, etc.
TK&S	Toye Kenning & Spencer	20th C	Prolific makers of regalia, medals, etc.
T S	Thomas Shaw	Late 1st ¼/2nd ¼ 19th C	Boxes, etc.
TW	Thomas Willmore	Late 18th/Early 19th C	Buckle maker
V.B & S	Vale Bros & Sermon	Late 19th/Early 20th C	Manufacturer
Y&W	Yapp & Woodward	Mid 19th C	Boxes, etc.
Z	A & J Zimmerman	20th C	

CHAPTER III
Chester

Cycles of Hallmarks

APPROXIMATE DATE	MARK			
1678				
c.1683				
1685				
c.1697-1701				

The above is a selection of early Chester marks. Prior to the mid 17th century makers' marks only appear to have been struck. See *Jackson's* pp.389/390 for full list.

CHESTER HALLMARKS
CYCLE I

DATE	CITY ARMS	CITY CREST	DATE LETTER
1 Feb. 1686-87 -2 June 1690			
2 June 1690-92	"	"	
1692-93 or 1694	"	"	
1693 or 1694-1695	"	"	
1695	"	"	
1696	"	"	
Until 25 March 1697*	"	"	

* Date-letter conjectured.

CYCLE II

	BRIT- ANNIA	LION'S HEAD ERASED	CITY ARMS	DATE LETTER
29 Sept. 1701				A
1702-7 April 1703	"	"	"	B
7 April 1703-4	"	"	"	C
1704-5	"	"	"	D
1705-6	"	"	"	E
1706-7	"	"	"	F
1707-8	"	"	"	G
1708-9	"	"	"	H
1709-10	"	"	"	I
1710-11	"	"	"	K
9 July 1711- 9 July 1712	"	"	"	L
1712-13	"	"	"	M
1713-14		"	"	N
1714-15	"	"	"	O
1715-16	"	"	"	P
1716-17	"	"	"	Q
1717-18	"	"	"	R
1718-19	"	"	"	S
1719-1 June 1720	"	"	"	T

	LION PASSANT	LEOPARD'S HEAD	CITY ARMS	DATE LETTER
2 June 1720- 9 July 1720				T
9 July 1720-21	"	"	"	U
1721-22	"	"	"	V
1722-23	"	"	"	W
1723-24	"	"	"	X
9 July 1724-25*	"	"	"	Y
1725-26*	"	"		Z

CYCLE III

	LION PASSANT	LEOPARD'S HEAD	CITY ARMS	DATE LETTER
9 July 1726-* † 10 July 1727				A
10 July 1727-* † 9 July 1728	"	"	"	B
9 July 1728-* † 9 July 1729	"	"	"	C
9 July 1729- † 9 July 1730		"	"	D
9 July 1730- † 9 July 1731		"	"	E
9 July 1731- 10 July 1732	"		"	F
10 July 1732- 9 July 1733	"	"	"	G
9 July 1733- 9 July 1734	"	"	"	H
9 July 1734- 9 July 1735	"	"	"	J
9 July 1735- 9 July 1736	"		"	K
9 July 1736- 9 July 1737	"	"	"	L
9 July 1737- 10 July 1738	"	"	"	M
10 July 1738- 9 July 1739	"	"	"	N
9 July 1739- 9 July 1740	"	"	"	O
9 July 1740-§ 9 July 1741	"	"	"	P
9 July 1741- 9 July 1742	"	"	"	Q
9 July 1742-‡ 9 July 1743	"	"	"	R
9 July 1743- 9 July 1744	"	"	"	S
9 July 1744- 9 July 1745	"	"	"	T
9 July 1745- 9 July 1746	"	"	"	U
9 July 1746- 9 July 1747	"	"	"	V
9 July 1747- 9 July 1748	"	"	"	W
9 July 1748- 10 July 1749	"	"	"	X
10 July 1749- 9 July 1750	"	"	"	Y
9 July 1750- 9 July 1751	"	"	"	Z

* Alternative lion passant 1724-29   † Alternative leopard's head 1726-31

§ Alternative City Arms used in 1741   ‡ A short bodied lion with undipped corners to the punch may be found in 1742.

CYCLE IV

	LION PASSANT	LEOPARD'S HEAD*	CITY ARMS	DATE LETTER
9 July 1751-9 July 1752	☙	☙	☙	**a**
9 July 1752-20 July 1753	"	"	"	**b**
20 July 1753-20 July 1754	"	"	"	**c**
20 July 1754-21 July 1755	"	"	"	**d**
21 July 1755-21 July 1756	"	"	"	**e**
21 July 1756-20 July 1757	"	"	"	**f**
20 July 1757-^{s}20 July 1758	"	"	"	**g**
20 July 1758-20 July 1759	"	"	"	**h**
20 July 1759-20 July 1760	"	"	"	**i**
20 July 1760-20 July 1761	"	"	☙	**k**
20 July 1761-20 July 1762	"	"	"	**l**
20 July 1762-20 July 1763	☙	"	"	**m**
20 July 1763-20 July 1764	"	"	"	**n**
20 July 1764-20 July 1765	"	"	"	**o**
20 July 1765-20 July 1766	"	"	"	**p**
20 July 1766-20 July 1767	"	"	"	**q**
20 July 1767-20 July 1768	"	"	"	**R**
20 July 1768-20 July 1769	"	"	"	**S**
20 July 1769-20 July 1770	"	"	"	**T**
20 July 1770-20 July 1771	"	"	"	**U**
20 July 1771-20 July 1772	"	"	"	**V**
20 July 1772-20 July 1773	"	"	"	**W**
20 July 1773-20 July 1774	"	"	"	**X**
20 July 1774-20 July 1775	"	"	"	**Y**
20 July 1775-20 July 1776	"	"	"	**Z**

CYCLE V

	LION PASSANT	LEOPARD'S HEAD*	CITY ARMS	DATE LETTER	DUTY MARK
20 July 1776-20 July 1777	☙	☙	☙	**a**	
20 July 1777-20 July 1778	"	"	"	**b**	
20 July 1778-20 July 1779 †	"	☙	☙	**c**	
20 July 1779-20 July 1780 †	"	"	"	**d**	
20 July 1780-20 July 1781 †	"	"	"	**e**	
20 July 1781-20 July 1782 †	☙	"	"	**f**	
20 July 1782-20 July 1783	"	☙	☙	**g**	
20 July 1783-31 Nov. 1784	"	"	"	**h**	
1 Dec. 1784-28 Jan. 1785 ‡	"	"	"	"	☙
28 Jan. 1785-20 July 1785	"	"	"	**i**	"
20 July 1785-20 July 1786	"	"	"	**k**	"
" " "	"	"	"	"	☙
20 July 1786-20 July 1787	"	"	"	**l**	"
20 July 1787-20 July 1788	"	"	"	**m**	"
20 July 1788-20 July 1789	"	"	"	**n**	"
20 July 1789-20 July 1790	"	"	"	**o**	"
20 July 1790-20 July 1791	"	"	"	**p**	"
20 July 1791-20 July 1792	"	"	"	**q**	"
20 July 1792-20 July 1793	"	"	"	**r**	"
20 July 1793-20 July 1794	"	"	"	**s**	"
20 July 1794-20 July 1795 **	"	☙	"	**t**	"
20 July 1795-20 July 1796 **	"	"	"	**U**	"
20 July 1796-[20 July 1797]	"	"	"	**V**	"

* The leopard's head punch used 1735-1778 becomes very worn during this period.

^{s} Alternative City Arms used in 1757.

† Alternative leopard's head 1778-82.

‡ Duty mark incuse.

** Leopard's head as in 1782 may be found.

CYCLE VI

	LION PASSANT	LEOPARD'S HEAD	CITY ARMS	DATE LETTER	DUTY* MARK
[20 July 1797-1798]				A	
[20 July 1798-20 July 1799]	"	"	"	B	"
[20 July 1799-20 July 1800] †			"	C	"
[20 July 1800-20 July 1801] †	"	"	"	D	"
[20 July 1801-20 July 1802]	"	"	"	E	"
1802-1803	"	"	"	F	"
1803-1804	"	"	"	G	"
1804-1805	"	"	"	H	"
1805-1806	"	"	"	I	"
1806-1807				K	"
1807-5 July 1808	"	"	"	L	"
5 July 1808-5 July 1809	"	"	"	M	"
5 July 1809-1810	"			N	"
1810-5 July 1811	"	"	"	O	"
5 July 1811-1812	"	"	"	P	"
1812-5 July 1813	"	"	"	Q	"
5 July 1813-5 July 1814	"	"	"	R	"
5 July 1814-1815	"	"	"	S	"
1815-1816	"	"	"	T	"
1816-5 July 1817	"	"	"	U	"
5 July 1817-5 July 1818	"	"	"	V	"

CYCLE VII

	LION PASSANT	LEOPARD'S HEAD	CITY ARMS	DATE LETTER	DUTY* MARK
5 July 1818-7 Sept. 1819				A	
7 Sept. 1819-10 May 1820			"	B	"
10 May 1820-8 Nov. 1821	"	"	"	C	"
8 Nov. 1821-5 July 1823 ‡	"		"	D	"
5 July 1823-5 July 1824	"	"		E	"
5 July 1824-5 July 1825§	"		"	F	"
5 July 1825-5 July1826§	"	"	"	G	"
5 July 1826-5 July 1827§	"	"	"	H	"
5 July 1827-5 July 1828§	"	"	"	I	"
5 July 1828-5 July 1829§	"	"	"	K	"
5 July 1829-5 July 1830§		"	"	L	"
5 July 1830-5 July 1831§	"	"	"	M	"
5 July 1831-5 July 1832§	"	"	"	N	"
5 July 1832-5 July 1833§	"	"	"	O	"
5 July 1833-5 July 1834	"	"		P	"
5 July 1834-5 July 1835		"	"	Q	"
5 July 1835-5 July 1836	"	"	"	R	"
5 July 1836-5 July 1837	"	"	"	S	"
5 July 1837-5 July 1838	"	"		T	
5 July 1838-5 July 1839	"	"	"	U	"

*   Other known duty marks used between 1797-1837.

†   The lion passant guardant and leopard's head as used in 1797 may still be found.

‡   Lion also appears in plain rectangular punch in 1821-23. The leopard's head may be found as in 1819. There was also a variant of the city arms.

§   Leopard's head may be found as in 1821.

CYCLE VIII

	LION PASSANT	TOWN MARK	DATE LETTER	DUTY MARK
1839-40	🦁	🛡	**A**	☺
1840-41	"	"	**B**	"
1841-42	"	"	**C**	"
1842-43	"	"	**D**	"
1843-44	"	"	**E**	"
1844-45	"	"	**f**	"
1845-46	"	"	**G**	"
1846-47	"	"	**H**	"
1847-48	"	"	**I**	"
1848-49	"	"	**K**	"
1849-50	"	"	**L**	"
1850-51	"	"	**M**	"
1851-52	"	"	**N**	"
1852-53	"	"	**O**	"
1853-54	"	"	**P**	"
1854-55	"	"	**Q**	"
1855-56	"	"	**R**	"
1856-57	"	"	**S**	"
1857-58	"	"	**T**	"
1858-59	"	"	**U**	"
1859-60	"	"	**V**	"
1860-61	"	"	**W**	"
1861-62	"	"	**X**	"
1862-63	"	"	**Y**	"
1863-64	"	"	**Z**	"

CYCLE IX

	LION PASSANT	TOWN MARK	DATE LETTER	DUTY MARK
1864-65	🦁	🛡	**a**	☺
1865-66	"	"	**b**	"
1866-67*	"	"	**c**	"
1867-68	"	"	**d**	"
1868-69	"	"	**e**	"
1869-70	"	"	**f**	"
1870-71	"	"	**g**	"
1871-72	"	"	**h**	"
1872-73	"	"	**i**	"
1873-74	"	"	**k**	"
1874-75	"	"	**l**	"
1875-76	"	"	**m**	"
1876-77	"	"	**n**	"
1877-78	"	"	**o**	"
1878-79	"	"	**p**	"
1879-80	"	"	**q**	"
1880-81	"	"	**r**	"
1881-82	"	"	**s**	"
1882-83	"	"	**t**	"
1883-84	"	"	**u**	"

* **F**   Struck in addition to the above on imported wares 1867-1904.

CYCLE X

	LION PASSANT	TOWN MARK	DATE LETTER	DUTY MARK
1884-85			**A**	
1885-86	"	"	**B**	"
1886-87	"	"	**C**	"
1887-88	"	"	**D**	"
1888-89	"	"	**E**	"
1889-1 May 1890	"	"	**F**	"
2 May 1890 5 July 1890	"	"	"	
1890-91	"	"	**G**	
1891-92	"	"	**H**	
1892-93	"	"	**I**	
1893-94	"	"	**K**	
1894-95	"	"	**L**	
1895-96	"	"	**M**	
1896-97	"	"	**N**	
1897-98	"	"	**O**	
1898-99	"	"	**P**	
1899-1900	"	"	**Q**	
1900-1	"	"	**R**	

CYCLE XI

	LION PASSANT GUARDANT	TOWN MARK	DATE LETTER
EDW.VII 1901-2			*A*
1902-3	"	"	*B*
1903-4	"	"	*C*
1904-5	"	"	*D*
1905-6	"	"	*E*
1906-7	"	"	*F*
1907-8	"	"	*G*
1908-9	"	"	*H*
1909-10	"	"	*I*
GEO.V 1910-11	"	"	*K*
1911-12	"	"	*L*
1912-13	"	"	*M*
1913-14	"	"	*N*
1914-15	"	"	*O*
1915-16	"	"	*P*
1916-17	"	"	*Q*
1917-18	"	"	*R*
1918-19	"	"	*S*
1919-20	"	"	*T*
1920-21	"	"	*U*
1921-22	"	"	*V*
1922-23	"	"	*W*
1923-24	"	"	*X*
1924-25	"	"	*Y*
1925-26	"	"	*Z*

CYCLE XII

	LION PASSANT GUARDANT	TOWN MARK	DATE LETTER
1926-27	🦁	🛡	**a**
1927-28	"	"	**k**
1928-29	"	"	**c**
1929-30	"	"	**d**
1930-31	"	"	**e**
1931-32	"	"	**ff**
1932-33	"	"	**G**
1933-34	"	"	**h**
1934-35*	"	"	**i**
1935-36*	"	"	**k**
EDW.VIII 1936-37	"	"	**l**
GEO.VI 1937-38	"	"	**m**
1938-39	"	"	**n**
1939-40	"	"	**o**
1940-41	"	"	**p**
1941-42	"	"	**q**
1942-43	"	"	**r**
1943-44	"	"	**s**
1944-45	"	"	**t**
1945-46	"	"	**u**
1946-47	"	"	**v**
1947-48	"	"	**w**
1948-49	"	"	**x**
1949-50	"	"	**y**
1950-51	"	"	**z**

CYCLE XIII

	LION PASSANT GUARDANT	TOWN MARK	DATE LETTER
1951-52	🦁	🛡	**A**
ELIZ.II 1952-53 †	"	"	**B**
1953-54 †	"	"	**C**
1954-55	"	"	**D**
1955-56	"	"	**E**
1956-57	"	"	**F**
1957-58	"	"	**G**
1958-59	"	"	**H**
1959-60	"	"	**J**
1960-61	"	"	**K**
1961-62	"	"	**L**
1 July- 24 Aug. 1962	"	"	**M**

*   Jubilee mark optional.

†   Coronation mark optional. 🦁

The Chester Assay Office closed on 24 August, 1962.

MARKS ON CHESTER GOLD WARES PRIOR TO 1932

Examples for 1907

22ct.	👑	22	▶	𝒢
18ct.	👑	18	▶	𝒢
15ct.	▶	15	·625	𝒢
12ct.	12	·5	▶	𝒢
9ct.	▶	9	·375	𝒢

IMPORT MARKS (Post 1904)

From 1904 to the closure of the Assay Office in 1962 an 'acorn and two leaves' replaced the 'letter F' and the 'town mark' for both gold (canted square punch) and silver (oval punch).

	IMPORTED GOLD		
22ct.	🌰	22 ·916	+ date letter and sponsor's mark
20ct.	"	20 ·833	"
18ct.	"	18 ·75	"
15ct.	"	15 ·625	"
12ct.	"	12 ·5	"
9ct.	"	9 ·375	"

	IMPORTED SILVER		
Britannia	🌰	·9584	+ date letter and sponsor's mark
Sterling	"	·925	"

1932-62

The alteration in gold standards in 1932 led to the following changes to the gold import marks.

	IMPORTED GOLD		
22ct.	🌰	22 916	+ date letter and sponsor's mark
18ct.	"	18 750	"
14ct.	"	14 585	"
9ct.	"	9 375	"

Chester Makers' Marks

One family, the Richardsons, produced the majority of silver in 18th C Chester. Since they nearly all were Richardsons, and variations of makers' mark RR are numerous, a selection is included below. (Reference to both *Jackson's* Chester section and Maurice Ridgway's *Chester Silver 1727-1837* is strongly recommended.) After the Richardsons the Lowes are the most prolific and are still in Chester today.

MARK	MAKER	PERIOD	COMMENTS
GL	George Lowe I	Late 18th/Early 19th C	Large variety of plate
G.L	George Lowe II	Late 1st ¼/Early 2nd ¼ 19th C	Large variety of plate
GL	George Lowe, jun	Mid 19th C	Large variety of plate
J.L	John Lowe	Mid 19th C	Flatware
JS	John Sutter (Liverpool)	2nd ¼ 19th C	Flatware
Ri	Richard Richardson I	1st ¼ 18th C	Large variety of plate
RL	Robert Lowe	Mid 19th C	Flatware
RR	Richard Richardson I & II	Early 2nd ¼ 18th C	Large variety of plate
RR	Richard Richardson II	Mid 18th C	Large variety of plate
RR	" "	" "	
R·R	" "	" "	
RR	Richard Richardson II & III	3rd ¼ 18th C	Large variety of plate
RR	Richard Richardson IV	4th ¼ 18th C	Large variety of plate

Note: Much work from the mid 19th C and on is found with Chester marks. The vast majority of this was only hallmarked there, not made there. Most originated from manufacturing centres of which Birmingham was the most important.

CHAPTER IV

Dublin

Cycles of Hallmarks

Where more than one version of a mark is shown in the following cycles, these are variations and will not be found together on one piece.

CYCLE I

	HARP CROWNED	DATE LETTER
CHAS.I 1636		
1638-39*		𝔸
1639-40*		𝔹
1640-41	"	ℂ
1641-42	"	𝔻
1642-43		E
1643-44		F
1644-45*		G
1645-46*		H
1646-47*		I
1647-48*		K
1648-49*		L
COMWTH. 1649-50		M
1650-51		N
1651-52		O
1652-53		P
1653-54		Q
1654-55*		ℝ
1655-56*		𝕊
1656-57*	"	𝕋
1657-58		U

CYCLE II

	HARP CROWNED	DATE LETTER
1658-59		a
1659-60*		𝕓
CHAS.II 1660-61		c
1661-62		d
1662-63		e
1663-64*		𝖋
1664-65	"	𝕘
1665-66		h
1666-67		i
1667-68		k
1668-69		l
1669-70		m
1670-71		n
1671-72		𝕠
1672-73		p
1673-74		q
1674-75		r
1675-76		s
1676-77		t
1677-78		u

* Date letter recorded.

CYCLE III

	HARP CROWNED	DATE LETTER
1678-79		𝕬
1679-80		𝕭
1680-81		𝕮
1681-82	"	𝕯
1682-83	"	𝕰
1683-84		𝕱
JAS.II 1685-87		𝕲
1688-93		𝕳 𝕴
WM.III 1694-95		𝕶
1696-98	"	𝕷
1699-1700		𝕸
1700-1		𝕹
1701-2		𝕺
ANNE 1702-3		𝕻
1703-4		𝕼 𝕹
1704-5		𝕽
1706-7		𝕾
1708-9		𝕿
1710-11		𝖀
1712-13		𝖂
GEO.I 1714-15	"	𝖄
1715-16		𝖅
1716-17		𝖅

CYCLE IV

	HARP CROWNED	DATE LETTER
1717-18		𝕬
		"
1718-19	"	𝕭
1719-20		𝕮
		𝕮

CYCLE V

	HIBERNIA	HARP CROWNED	DATE LETTER
1720-21		🏴	A
1721-22		"	B
1722-23		"	C
1723-24		"	D / D
1724-25		🏴	E
1725-26		"	F
1726-27		"	G
GEO.II 1727-28		🏴	H
1728-29		"	J
1729-30		🏴	K
1730-31		"	L
1731-32	🏴	🏴	L
1732-33	🏴	"	M
1733-34	"	"	N
1734-35	🏴	🏴	O
1735-36	"	"	P
1736-37	"	"	Q
1737-38	"	"	R
1738-39	"	"	S
1739-40	"	"	T
1740-41	"	"	U
1741-43	"	"	W / TB
1743-44	"	"	X
1745	"	"	Y
1746	"	"	Z

CYCLE VI

	HIBERNIA	HARP CROWNED	DATE LETTER
1747	🏴	🏴	A
1748	"	"	B
1749	"	🏴	C
1750	"	"	D
1751-52	"	🏴	E E
1752-53	🏴 *	"	F
1753-54	"	"	G
1754-56	🏴	"	H
1757	"	"	J
1758	"	🏴	K
1759	"	"	L
GEO.III 1760	"	"	M
1761	"	"	N
1762	"	🏴	O
1763	"	"	P
1764	"	"	Q
1765	"	"	R
1766	"	"	S
1767	"	🏴	T
1768	"	"	U
1769	🏴	🏴	W
1770	"	"	X
1771	"	🏴	Y
1772	"	"	Z

* The Hibernia stamp of this form was used between 1752 and 1754 as well as one of oval outline.

CYCLE VII

	HIBERNIA	HARP CROWNED	DATE LETTER
1773	🝑	🝑	**A**
1774	"	"	**B**
1775	"	"	**C**
1776*	"	🝑	**D**
1777	"	"	**E**
1778	"	"	**F**
1779*	"	"	**G**
1780	"	"	**H**
1781	"	"	**I**
1782	"	"	**K**
1783	"	"	**L**
1784	"	"	**M**
1785	"	"	**N**
1786	"	"	**O**
1787	"	"	**P**
	🝑	🝑	"
1788	"	"	**Q**
1789	"	"	**R**
1790	"	"	**S**
1791	"	"	**T**
1792	"	"	**U**
1793	"	"	**W**
1794	🝑	🝑	**X**
1795	"	"	**Y**
1796	"	"	**Z**

CYCLE VIII

	HIBER-NIA	HARP CROWNED	DATE LETTER	DUTY MARK
1797	🝑	🝑	**A**	
1798	"	"	**B**	
1799	"	"	**C**	
1800	"	"	**D**	
1801	"	"	**E**	
1802	"	"	**F**	
1803	"	"	**G**	
1804	"	"	**H**	
1805	"	"	**I**	
1806	🝑	🝑	**K**	
1807	"	"	**L**	🝑
1808	"	"	**M**	"
1809	"	"	**NN**	🝑

	DATE LETTER	HARP CROWNED	HIBER-NIA	DUTY MARK
1810	**OO**	🝑	🝑	"
1811	**P**	"	"	"
1812	**Q**	"	"	"
1813	**R**	"	"	"
1814	**S**	"	"	"
1815	**T**	"	"	"
1816	**U**	"	"	"
1817	**W**	"	"	"
1818	**X**	"	"	"
1819	**Y**	"	"	"
GEO.IV 1820	**Z**	"	"	"

* D and G are sometimes found without pellet.

CYCLE IX

	DATE LETTER	HARP CROWNED	HIBER-NIA	DUTY MARK
1821	A	[mark]	[mark]	[mark]
1822	B	"	"	[mark]
1823	C	"	"	"
1824	D	"	"	"
1825-26	E e	"	"	[mark]
1826-27	F	"	"	[mark]
1827-28	G	[mark]	[mark]	[mark]
1828-29	H	[mark]	[mark]	[mark]
1829-30	I I	[mark]	[mark]	[mark]
WM.IV 1830-31	K	[mark]	[mark]	[mark]
1831-32	L	[mark]	[mark]	[mark]
1832-33	M	[mark]	[mark]	[mark]
1833-34	N N	[mark]	[mark]	"
1834-35*	O O	[mark]	[mark]	[mark]
1835-36	P P	"	"	"
1836-37	Q Q	"	"	"
VICT. 1837-38	R R	"	"	"
1838-39	S	[mark]	[mark]	[mark]
1839-40	T	[mark]	[mark]	"
1840-41	U U	"	"	"
1841-42	V	"	"	"
1842-43	W	[mark]	[mark]	"
1843-44	X	[mark]	"	"
1844-45	Y	[mark]	[mark]	"
1845-46	Z	[mark]	[mark]	"

CYCLE X

	HIBER-NIA	HARP CROWNED	DATE LETTER	DUTY MARK
1846-47	[mark]	[mark]	a	[mark]
1847-48	"	"	b	"
1848-49	"	"	c	"
1849-50	"	"	d	"
1850-51	"	"	e	"
1851-52	"	"	f f	"
1852-53	"	"	g g	"
1853-54	"	"	h h	"
1854-55	"	"	j	"
1855-56	"	"	k	"
1856-57	"	"	l	"
1857-58	"	"	m	"
1858-59	"	"	n	"
1859-60	"	"	o	"
1860-61	"	"	p	"
1861-62	"	"	q	"
1862-63	"	"	r	"
1863-64	"	"	s	"
1864-65	[mark]	"	t	"
1865-66	"	"	u	"
1866-67	"	"	v	"
1867-68	"	"	w	"
1868-69	"	"	x	"
1869-70	"	"	y	"
1870-71	"	"	z	"

CYCLE XI

	HARP CROWNED	HIBER-NIA	DATE LETTER	DUTY MARK
1871-72	🏵	🏛	**A**	🌐
1872-73	"	"	**B**	"
1873-74	"	"	**C**	"
1874-75	"	"	**D**	"
1875-76	"	"	**E**	"
1876-77	"	"	**F**	"
1877-78	"	"	**G**	"
1878-79	"	"	**H**	"
1879-80	"	"	**I**	"
1880-81	"	"	**K**	"
1881-82	"	"	**L**	"
1882-83	"	"	**M**	"
1883-84	"	"	**N**	"
1884-85	"	"	**O**	"
1885-86	"	"	**P**	"
1886-87	"	"	**Q**	"
1887-88	"	"	**R**	"
1888-89	"	"	**S**	"
1889-90	"	"	**T**	"
1890-91	"	"	**U**	
1891-92	"	"	**V**	
1892-93	"	"	**W**	
1893-94	"	"	**X**	
1894-95	"	"	**Y**	
1895-96	"	"	**Z**	

CYCLE XII

	HARP CROWNED	HIBER-NIA	DATE LETTER
1896-97	🏵	🏛	**A**
1897-98	"	"	**B**
1898-99	"	"	**C**
1899-1900	"	"	**D**
1900-1	"	"	**E**
EDW.VII 1901-2	"	"	**F**
1902-3	"	"	**G**
1903-4	🏵	🏛	**H**
1904-5	"	"	**I**
1905-6	"	"	**K**
1906-7	"	"	**L**
1907-8	"	"	**M**
1908-9	"	"	**N**
1909-10	"	"	**O**
1910-11	"	"	**P**
1911-12	"	"	**Q**
1912-13	"	"	**R**
1913-14	"	"	**S**
1914-15	"	"	**T**
1915-16	"	"	**U**

CYCLE XIII

	HARP CROWNED	HIBERNIA	DATE LETTER
1916	🏷	🏷	a
1917	"	"	b
1918	"	"	c
1919	"	"	d
1920	"	"	e
1921	"	"	f
1922	"	"	g
1923	"	"	h
1924	"	"	i
1925	"	"	k
1926	"	"	l
1927	"	"	m
1928	"	"	n
1929	"	"	o
1930-31	"	"	p
1932	"	"	q
1933	"	"	r
1934	"	"	s
1935	"	"	t
1936	"	"	u
1937	"	"	v
1938	"	"	w
1939	"	"	x
1940	"	"	y
1941	"	"	z

CYCLE XIV

	HIBERNIA	HARP CROWNED	DATE LETTER
1942	🏷	🏷	A
1943	"	"	B
1944	"	"	C
1945	🏷	🏷	D
1946	"	"	E
1947	"	"	F
1948	"	"	G
1949	🏷	🏷	H
1950	"	"	I
1951	"	"	J
1952	"	"	K
1953	"	"	L
1954	"	"	M
1955	"	"	N
1956	"	"	O
1957	"	"	P
1958	"	"	Q
1959	"	"	R
1960	"	"	S
1961	"	"	T
1962	"	"	U
1963	"	"	V
1964	"	"	W
1965	"	"	X
1966*	🏷	"	Y
1967	"	"	Z

* Jubilee mark.

CYCLE XV

	HARP CROWNED	HIBER-NIA	DATE LETTER
1968	🦁	🏛	**a**
1969	"	"	**b**
1970	"	"	**c**
1971	🦁	🏛	**d**
1972	"	"	**e**
1973*	"	🏛	**f**
1974	"	"	**g**
1975	"	"	**h**
1976	"	"	**i**
1977	"	"	**l**
1978	"	"	**m**
1979	"	"	**n**
1980	"	"	**o**
1981	"	"	**p**
1982	"	"	**R**
1983	"	"	**s**
1984	"	"	**t**
1985	"	"	**u**

CYCLE XVI

	HARP CROWNED	HIBER-NIA	DATE LETTER
1986	🦁	🏛	**A**
1987**	"	"	**B**
1988 †	"	"	**C**
1989	"	"	**D**
1990	"	"	**E**
1991	"	"	**F**

*   Additional mark to commemorate Ireland's entry into the European Community.

**   To denote the 350th Anniversary of the founding of the Company of Goldsmiths, the Company authorised the striking of a special mark to be put on all items of Irish manufactured gold, silver and platinum, other than jewellery and watch cases, manufactured and hallmarked during the period, 1 January to 31 December 1987. The mark consists of a shield from the Coat of Arms of the Company and appears in addition to the appropriate regular hallmarks.

†   To denote the Dublin City Millennium Year the Company of Goldsmiths authorised the striking of a special mark to be put on all items of Irish manufactured gold, silver and platinum, other than jewellery and watch cases, manufactured and hallmarked during the period, 1 January to 31 December 1988. The mark represents the Dublin Coat of Arms and appears in addition to the appropriate regular hallmarks.

MARK	MAKER	PERIOD	COMMENTS
	Abel Ram	2nd ½ 17th C	Fine work
	" "	" "	
	" "	" "	
	Charles Leslie	2nd ¼ 18th C	One of the finest of all makers
	Charles Townsend	Late 18th C	Good work
	Daniel Egan	Early 19th C	Good maker
	David King	Early 18th C	Fine maker
	" "	" "	
	Isaac D'Olier	Mid 18th C	Good maker
	John Hamilton	1st ½ 18th C	Important maker
	James Keating	Late 18th C	Many boxes
	John Laughlin	Mid 18th C	Interesting maker
	James Le Bass	Early 19th C	Good maker
	Joseph Stoaker (or John Slicer)	2nd ½ 17th C	Fine work
	John Pittar	Late 18th C	Good work
	J R Neill	Mid 19th C	Important retail firm
	John Tuite	Early 18th C	Moved to London where he used the same mark
	Joseph Walker	Late 17th/Early 18th C	Important maker
	" "	" "	
LAW	William Law	Late 18th/Early 19th C	Good work
	Michael Keating	Late 18th C	Good work
	MK " "	" "	
	Matthew Walker	2nd ¼ 18th C	Good maker

MARK	MAKER	PERIOD	COMMENTS
MW	Matthew Walsh	Late 18th C	Good work
MW	Michael Walsh	2nd ½ 18th C	Good work
MW&S	M West & Sons	19th C	Important retail firm
NEILL	J R Neill	Mid 19th C	Important retail firm
RC	Robert Calderwood	Mid 18th C	Very important maker
R·C	" "	" "	
R·C	" "	" "	
B	Thomas Bolton	Late 17th/Early 18th C	Important maker
B	" "	" "	
TW	Thomas Walker	1st ½/Mid 18th C	Very fine maker
TW	" "	" "	
TW	" "	" "	
W&Cº	Alderman West & Co	19th C	Important retail firm
W&R	Weir & Rogers	Late 19th C	Retailers
W&S	West & Son	Late 19th C	Important retail firm
W&S	" "	" "	
W&S	" "	Early 20th C	
WB	William Bond	2nd ½ 18th C	Prolific maker
WEST	Alderman West	Early 19th C	Important retail firm
WL	William Law	Late 18th/Early 19th C	Good work
WT	William Townsend	Mid 18th C	Good work
WT	" "	" "	
WW	William Williamson	2nd ¼ 18th C	Fine maker

Edinburgh

Cycles of Hallmarks

Pre 1681

	TOWN MARK CASTLE	DEACON'S MARK
1556-67 or 1561-62		
1563-64	"	
1565-67	"	
c.1575?	"	
1576		
1577-79		
1585-86	"	
1592-93	"	
1598-1601	"	
1603-4		
1608-10	"	
1611-13		
1613-21		
1617	"	
c.1617		
1617-19	"	
1633		
1637-39		

	TOWN MARK CASTLE	DEACON'S MARK
1640-42		
1642	"	
1643		"
1644-46	"	
1648-57	"	
c.1650?	"	
1651-59	"	
1660	"	
1663-81	"	
1665	"	
1665-67	"	
1669-75	"	
1675-77	"	

CYCLE I

	TOWN MARK CASTLE	ASSAY MASTER'S MARK	DATE LETTER
1681-82	castle	B	a
1682-83	"	B	b
1683-84	"	"	c
1684-85	"	"	d
1685-86	"	"	e
1686-87	"	"	f
1687-88*	"	"	g
1688-89	"	"	h
WM.& MY. 1689-90	"	"	i
1690-91	"	"	k
1691-92	"	"	l
1692-93	"	"	m
1693-94	"	"	n
1694-95	"	"	o
WM.III 1695-96	"	"	p
1696-97	"	"	q
1697-98 †	"	P**	r
1698-99	castle	"	s
1699-1700	"	"	t
1700-1	"	"	u
1701-2	"	"	w
ANNE 1702-3	"	"	x
1703-4	"	"	y
1704-5	"	"	z

* Date letter variation: g   1687-88

† Date letter variation: 1697-98

** Penman did not become Assay Master until 13 Sept., 1697.

CYCLE II

	TOWN MARK CASTLE	ASSAY MASTER'S MARK	DATE LETTER
1705-6	castle	P	A
1706-7	"	"	B
1707-8	"	EP	C
1708-9	"	"	D
1709-10	"	"	E
1710-11	"	"	F
1711-12	"	"	G
			G
1712-13	"	"	H
1713-14	"	"	I
GEO.I 1714-15	castle	"	K
1715-16	"	"	L
1716-17	"	"	M
1717-18	"	"	N
			N
	castle	EP	N
1718-19	"	"	O
		EP	P
1719-20	castle	"	P
		EP	P
1720-21	"	"	Q
1721-22	"	"	R
1722-23	"	"	S
1723-24	"	"	T
1724-25	"	"	U
1725-26	"	"	V
1726-27	"	"	W
GEO.II 1727-28	"	"	X
1728-29	"	"	Y
1729-30	"	"	Z
		AU	Z

CYCLE III

	TOWN MARK CASTLE	ASSAY MASTER'S MARK	DATE LETTER
1730-31	castle	AU	A
1731-32	"	"	B
1732-33	"	"	C
1733-34	"	"	D
1734-35	"	"	E
1735-36	"	"	F
1736-37	"	"	G
1737-38	castle	"	H
1738-39	"	"	I
1739-40	"	"	K
1740-41	"	" / GED	L
1741-42	"	"	M
1742-43	"	EL	N
1743-44	"	"	O
1744-45	castle	HG	P
1745-46	"	"	Q
1746-47	"	"	R
1747-48	"	"	S
1748-49	"	"	T
1749-50	"	"	U
1750-51	"	"	V
1751-52	"	"	W
1752-53	"	"	X
1753-54	"	"	Y
1754-55	"	"	Z

CYCLE IV

	TOWN MARK CASTLE	ASSAY MASTER'S MARK	DATE LETTER
1755-56	castle	HG	A
1756-57	"	"	B
1757-58	"	"	C
1758-59	"	"	D
1759-60	"	THISTLE	E
GEO.III 1760-61	"	"	F
1761-62	"	"	G
1762-63	"	"	H
1763-64	"	"	I
1764-65	"	"	K
1765-66	"	"	L
1766-67	"	"	M
1767-68	"	"	N
1768-69	"	"	O
1769-70	"	"	P
1770-71	"	"	Q
1771-72	"	"	R
1772-73	"	"	S
1773-74	"	"	T
1774-75	"	"	U
1775-76	"	"	V
1776-77	"	"	W
1777-78	"	"	X
1778-79	"	"	Y
1779-80	"	"	Z

CYCLE V

	DUTY MARK	TOWN MARK CASTLE	THISTLE	DATE LETTER
1780-81		⬚	⬚	**A**
1781-82		"	"	**B**
1782-83		"	"	**C**
1783-84		"	"	**D**
1784-85	⬚	"	"	**E**
1785-86	"	"	"	**F**
1786-88	⬚	"	"	**G**
1788-89	"	"	"	**H**
1789-90	"	"	"	**I**
				J
1790-91	"	"	"	**K**
1791-92	"	"	"	**L**
1792-93	"	"	"	**M**
1793-94	"	"	"	**N**
1794-95	"	"	"	**O**
1795-96	"	"	"	**P**
1796-97	"	"	"	**Q**
1797-98	⬚	"	"	**R**
1798-99	"	"	"	**S**
1799-1800	"	⬚	⬚	**T**
1800-1	"	"	"	**U**
1801-2	"	"	"	**V**
1802-3	"	⬚	"	**W**
1803-4	"	"	"	**X**
1804-5	"	"	"	**Y**
1805-6	"	"	"	**Z**

CYCLE VI

	DUTY MARK	TOWN MARK CASTLE	THISTLE	DATE LETTER
1806-7	⬚	⬚	⬚	**a**
1807-8	"	"	"	**b**
1808-9	"	"	"	**c**
1809-10	"	⬚	"	**d**
1810-11	"	"	"	**e**
1811-12	"	"	"	**f**
1812-13	"	"	"	**g**
1813-14	"	"	"	**h**
1814-15	"	"	"	**i**
1815-16	"	"	"	**j**
1816-17	"	"	"	**k**
1817-18	"	"	"	**l**
1818-19	"	"	"	**m**
1819-20	"	"	"	**n**
GEO.IV 1820-21	"	⬚	⬚	**o**
1821-22	"	"	"	**p**
1822-23	"	"	"	**q**
1823-24	⬚	"	"	**r**
1824-25	"	"	"	**s**
1825-26	"	"	"	**t**
1826-27	"	⬚	"	**u**
1827-28	"	"	"	**v**
1828-29	"	"	"	**w**
1829-30	"	"	"	**x**
WM.IV 1830-31	"	"	"	**y**
1831-32	"	"	"	**z**

CYCLE VII

	DUTY MARK	TOWN MARK CASTLE	THISTLE	DATE LETTER
1832-33	🂠	🏰	🂡	**A**
1833-34	"	"	"	**B**
1834-35	"	"	"	**C**
1835-36	"	"	"	**D**
1836-37	"	"	"	**E**
VICT. 1837-38	"	"	"	**F**
1838-39	"	"	"	**G**
1839-40	"	"	"	**H**
1840-41	"	"	"	**I**
1841-42	🂠	"	"	**K**
1842-43	"	"	"	**L**
1843-44	"	"	"	**M**
1844-45	"	"	"	**N**
1845-46	"	"	"	**O**
1846-47	"	"	"	**P**
1847-48	"	"	"	**Q**
1848-49	"	"	"	**R**
1849-50	"	"	"	**S**
1850-51	"	"	"	**T**
1851-52	"	"	"	**U**
1852-53	"	"	"	**V**
1853-54	"	"	"	**W**
1854-55	"	"	"	**X**
1855-56	"	"	"	**Y**
1856-57	"	"	"	**Z**

CYCLE VIII

	DUTY MARK	TOWN MARK CASTLE	THISTLE	DATE LETTER
1857-58	🂠	🏰	🂡	**A**
1858-59	"	"	"	**B**
1859-60	"	"	"	**C**
1860-61	"	"	"	**D**
1861-62	"	"	"	**E**
1862-63	"	"	"	**F**
1863-64	"	"	"	**G**
1864-65	"	"	"	**H**
1865-66	"	"	"	**I**
1866-67	"	"	"	**K**
1867-68*	"	"	"	**L**
1868-69	"	"	"	**M**
1869-70	"	"	"	**N**
1870-71	"	"	"	**O**
1871-72	"	"	"	**P**
1872-73	"	"	"	**Q**
1873-74	"	"	"	**R**
1874-75	"	"	"	**S**
1875-76	"	"	"	**T**
1876-77	"	"	"	**U**
1877-78	"	"	"	**V**
1878-79	"	"	"	**W**
1879-80	"	"	"	**X**
1880-81	"	"	"	**Y**
1881-82	"	"	"	**Z**

* **F** was struck on imported wares in addition to the marks shown from 1867-1904.

CYCLE IX

	DUTY MARK	TOWN MARK CASTLE	THISTLE	DATE LETTER
1882-83	🜚	🏰	🜲	**ɑ**
1883-84	"	"	"	**b**
1884-85	"	"	"	**c**
1885-86	"	"	"	**d**
1886-87	"	"	"	**e**
1887-88	"	"	"	**f**
1888-89	"	"	"	**g**
1889-90*	"	"	"	**h**
1890-91		🏰	🜲	**i**
1891-92		"	"	**k**
1892-93		"	"	**l**
1893-94		"	"	**m**
1894-95		"	"	**n**
1895-96		"	"	**o**
1896-97		"	"	**p**
1897-98		"	"	**q**
1898-99		"	"	**r**
1899-1900		"	"	**s**
1900-1		"	"	**t**
EDW.VII 1901-2		"	"	**u**
1902-3		"	"	**v**
1903-4 †		"	"	**w**
1904-5		"	"	**x**
1905-6		"	"	**z**

* Duty Mark is deleted as from 1890.

† 🇫 was struck on imported wares in addition to the marks shown from 1867-1904.

CYCLE X

	TOWN MARK CASTLE	THISTLE	DATE LETTER
1906-7	🏰	🜲	**A**
1907-8	"	"	**B**
1908-9ˢ	"	"	**C**
1909-10	"	"	**D**
GEO.V 1910-11	"	"	**E**
1911-12	"	"	**F**
1912-13	"	"	**G**
1913-14	"	"	**H**
1914-15	"	"	**I**
1915-16	"	"	**K**
1916-17	"	"	**L**
1917-18	"	"	**M**
1918-19	"	"	**N**
1919-20	"	"	**O**
1920-21	"	"	**P**
1921-22	"	"	**Q**
1922-23**	"	"	**R**
1923-24**	"	"	**S**
1924-25**	"	"	**T**
1925-26	"	"	**U**
1926-27	"	"	**V**
1927-28	"	"	**W**
1928-29**	"	"	**X**
1929-30	"	"	**Y**
1930-31	"	"	**Z**

ˢ New Britannia mark: 🜲

** Date letters exist for these years but are not recorded on the surviving registration plates.

CYCLE XI

	TOWN MARK CASTLE	THISTLE	DATE LETTER
1931-32			A
1932-33	"	"	B
1933-34	"	"	C
1934-35 †	"	"	D
1935-36 †	"	"	E
EDW.VIII 1936-37	"	"	F
GEO.VI 1937-38	"	"	G
1938-39	"	"	H
1939-40	"	"	J
1940-41			K
1941-42	"	"	L
1942-43	"	"	M
1943-44	"	"	N
1944-45	"	"	O
1945-46	"	"	P
1946-47	"	"	Q
1947-48	"	"	R
1948-49**	"	"	S
1949-50**	"	"	T
1950-51**	"	"	U
1951-52	"	"	V
ELIZ.II 1952-53§	"	"	W
1953-54§	"	"	X
1954-55	"	"	Y
1955-56	"	"	Z

CYCLE XII

	TOWN MARK CASTLE	THISTLE	DATE LETTER
1956-57			A
1957-58	"	"	B
1958-59	"	"	C
1959-60	"	"	D
1960-61	"	"	E
1961-62	"	"	F
1962-63	"	"	G
1963-64	"	"	H
1964-65	"	"	I
1965-66	"	"	K
1966-67	"	"	L
1967-68	"	"	M
1968-69	"	"	N
1969-70	"	"	O
1970-71	"	"	P
1971-72	"	"	Q
1972-73	"	"	R
1973-74	"	"	S

† Optional Jubilee Mark:

** Date letters exist for these years but are not recorded on the surviving registration plates.

§ Optional Coronation Mark:

CYCLE XIII

	TOWN MARK CASTLE	LION RAMPANT	DATE LETTER
1975 ‡	🏰	🦁	*A*
1976	"	"	*B*
1977 †	"	"	*C*
1978	"	"	*D*
1979	"	"	*E*
1980	"	"	*F*
1981	"	"	*G*
1982*	"	"	*H*
1983	"	"	*J*
1984	"	"	*K*
1985	"	"	*L*
1986	"	"	*M*
1987	"	"	*N*
1988	"	"	*O*
1989	"	"	*P*
1990	"	"	*Q*
1991	"	"	*R*

PLATINUM FROM 1982

	TOWN MARK CASTLE	PLATINUM MARK	DATE LETTER
Date as Above	🏰	⬡	*H*

‡   Britannia mark from 1975 on:

†   Optional Jubilee Mark: 🦁

GOLD MARKS

These follow almost exactly those used in London from 1798 on with the obvious substitution of the castle mark for the leopard's head (the sun in splendour for 22ct. was not used in Edinburgh).

IMPORT MARKS 1904-32

GOLD			IMPORTED SILVER			
22ct.		916	+ Date letter & sponsor's mark	Britannia		·9584	+ Date letter & sponsor's mark
20ct.	"	·833	"	Sterling	"	·925	"
18ct.	"	·75	"				
15ct.	"	·625	"				
12ct.	"	·5					
9ct.	"	375	"				

1932-74*

GOLD			SILVER
22ct.		916	+ Date letter & sponsor's mark	(As 1904-32)
18ct.	"	750	"	
14ct.	"	585	"	
9ct.	"	375	"	

From 1975 on

Platinum**		950	+ Date letter & sponsor's mark
Gold 22ct.		916	"
18ct.	"	750	"
14ct.	"	585	"
9ct.	"	375	"
Silver Britannia		958	"
Sterling	"	925	"

CONVENTION MARKS 1976 on

PRECIOUS METAL	ASSAY OFFICE MARK	COMMON CONTROL MARK	FINENESS MARK
Platinum**		950	950
Gold 18ct.	"	750	750
14ct.	"	585	585
9ct.	"	375	375
Silver (Sterling)	"	925	925

Convention marking on imported wares

PRECIOUS METAL	ASSAY OFFICE MARK	COMMON CONTROL MARK	FINENESS MARK
Platinum**		950	950
Gold 18ct.		750	750
14ct.	"	585	585
9ct.	"	375	375
Silver (Sterling)		925	925

*   In 1932 and from then on 14ct. replaced 15ct. and 12ct.

** Note platinum 1982 onwards

Since universally high standards were maintained by all the makers listed here, individual comments such as, 'Fine/Good maker' would be simply repetitive and are therefore not given.

MARK	MAKER	PERIOD	COMMENTS
AU	Archibald Ure	Early 18th C	
AZ	Alexander Zeigler	Late 18th/Early 19th C	
B&S	Brook & Son	Very late 19th C on	
E·L	Edward Lothian	2nd ¼ 18th C	
H&I	Hamilton & Inches	Late 19th C to present day	
H&I	" "	" "	
HB	Harry Beathune	Early 18th C	
HG	Hugh Gordon	2nd ¼ 18th C	
ID	James Dempster	Last ¼ 18th C	
IK	James Ker	2nd ¼ 18th C	
IM	James Mitchellsone	Early 18th C	
IZ	John Zeigler	Very late 18th/Early 19th C	
J&WM	James & William Marshall	1st ½ & Mid 19th C	
JC&C	J Crichton & Co	Late 19th C	
J&C°	" "	Very late 19th C on	
JN	James Nasmyth	2nd ¼ 19th C	Boxes
JM¹	J McKay	1st ½ 19th C	
JH&C°	James Nasmyth & Co	2nd ¼ 19th C	Boxes

MARK	MAKER	PERIOD	COMMENTS
K&D	Ker & Dempster	Mid 18th C	
L&R	Lothian & Robertson	Mid 18th C	
M&C	Mackay & Chisholm	Mid 19th C	
M&S	Marshall & Sons	2nd ¼ 19th C	
MK	Colin McKenzie	Late 17th/Early 18th C	
MY	Mungo Yorstoun	Early 18th C	
PC &S	P Cunningham & Son	Early 19th C	
PM	Patrick Murray	Early 18th C	
PR	Patrick Robertson	3rd ¼ 18th C	
RG	Robert Gordon	Mid 18th C	
RG &S	Robert Gray & Son (Glasgow)	Early 19th C	
T	James Taitt	Early 18th C	
TK	Thomas Ker	Early 18th C	
W& PC	William & Patrick Cunningham	Last ¼ 18th C	
WA	William Auld	Late 18th/Early 19th C	
WA	William Aytoun	c.2nd ¼ 18th C	
WC PC	William & Patrick Cunningham	Last ¼ 18th C	
WPC	W & P Cunningham	Late 18th C	
WZ	William Zeigler	1st ½ 19th C	

CHAPTER VI

Exeter

Cycles of Hallmarks

TABLE I

APPROXIMATE DATE	MARKS
1575	
1600	
1620	
1635	
1660	
1660	

The above is a small selection of the pre-1701 Exeter marks intended only to give an idea of the types of mark in use. See *Jackson's* pp.289/291 for full list.

CYCLE I

	CASTLE	BRIT-ANNIA	LION'S HEAD ERASED	DATE LETTER
1701-2	▨	▨	▨	**A**
ANNE 1702-3	▨	"	"	**B**
1703-4	▨	"	"	**C**
1704-5	"	"	"	**D**
1705-6	"	"	"	**E**
1706-7	"	"	"	**F**
1707-8	"	"	"	**G**
1708-9	▨	"	"	**H**
1709-10	▨	"	"	**I**
1710-11	"	"	"	**K**
1711-12	"	"	"	**L**
1712-13	"	"	"	**M**
1713-14	▨	"	"	**N**
GEO.I 1714-15	"	"	"	**O**
1715-16	"	"	"	**P**
1716-17	"	"	"	**Q**
1717-18	"	"	"	**R**
1718-19	"	"	"	**S**
1719-20	"	"	"	**T**
1720-21	"	"	"	**V**

	CASTLE	LEOPARD'S HEAD CROWNED	LION PASSANT	DATE LETTER
1720-21	▨	▨	▨	"
1721-22	"	"	"	**W**
1722-23	"	"	"	**X**
1723-24	"	"	"	**Y**
1724-25	"	"	"	**Z**

CYCLE II

	CASTLE	LEOPARD'S HEAD CROWNED	LION PASSANT	DATE LETTER
1725-26	▨	▨	▨	**a**
1726-27	"	"	"	**b**
GEO.II 1727-28	"	"	"	**c**
1728-29	"	"	"	**d**
1729-30	"	"	"	**e**
1730-31	"	"	"	**f**
1731-32	"	"	"	**g**
1732-33	"	"	"	**h**
1733-34	"	"	"	**i**
1734-35	"	"	"	**k**
1735-36	"	"	"	**l** / **L**
1736-37	"	"	"	**m**
1737-38	"	"	"	**n**
1738-39	"	"	"	**o**
1739-40	"	"	"	**p**
1740-41	"	"	"	**q**
1741-42	"	"	"	**r**
1742-43	"	"	"	**s**
1743-44	"	"	"	**t**
1744-45	"	"	"	**u**
1745-46	"	"	"	**w**
1746-47	"	"	"	**x**
1747-48	"	"	"	**y**
1748-49	"	"	"	**z**

CYCLE III

	CASTLE	LEOPARD'S HEAD CROWNED	LION PASSANT	DATE LETTER
1749-50	🏰	🦁	🦁	**A**
1750-51	"	"	"	**B**
1751-52	"	"	"	**C**
1752-53	"	"	"	**D**
1753-54	"	"	"	**E**
1754-55	"	"	"	**F**
1755-56	"	"	"	**G**
1756-57	"	"	"	**H**
1757-58	"	"	"	**I**
1758-59	"	"	"	**K**
1759-60	"	"	"	**L**
GEO.III 1760-61	"	"	"	**M**
1761-62	"	"	"	**N**
1762-63	"	"	"	**O**
1763-64	"	"	"	**P**
1764-65	"	"	"	**Q**
1765-66	"	"	"	**R**
1766-67	"	"	"	**S**
1767-68	"	"	"	**T**
1768-69	"	"	"	**U**
1769-70	"	"	"	**W**
1770-71	"	"	"	**X**
1771-72	"	"	"	**Y**
1772-73	"	"	"	**Z**

CYCLE IV

	CASTLE	LEOPARD'S HEAD CROWNED	LION PASSANT	DATE LETTER
1773-74	🏰	🦁	🦁	**A**
1774-75	"	"	"	B
1775-76	"	"	"	**C**
1776-77	"	"	"	D
1777-78	"	"	"	E
1778-79	"	"	🦁	**F**
1779-80	"		"	**G**
1780-81	"		"	H
1781-83	"		"	**I**
1783-84	"		"	**K**
1784-85	"	🖤	"	**L**
1785-86	"	"	"	**M**
1786-87	"	🖤	"	**N**
1787-88	"	"	"	**O**
1788-89	"	"	"	**P**
1789-90	"	"	"	**q**
1790-91	"	"	"	**r**
1791-92	"	"	"	**f**
1792-93	"	"	"	**t**
1793-94	"	"	"	u
1794-95	"	"	"	**W**
1795-96	"	"	"	**X**
1796-97	"	"	"	**y**

CYCLE V

	CASTLE	LION PASSANT	DATE LETTER	DUTY MARK
1797-8*	🏰	🦁	**A**	👤
1798-9 †	"	"	**B**	"
1799-1800	"	"	**C**	"
1800-1	"	"	**D**	"
1801-2	"	"	**E**	"
1802-3	"	"	**F**	"
1803-4	"	"	**G**	"
1804-5	"	"	**H**	"
1805-6	🏰	🦁	**I**	"
1806-7	"	"	**K**	"
1807-8	"	"	**L**	"
1808-9	"	"	**M**	"
1809-10	"	"	**N**	"
1810-11	"	"	**O**	"
1811-12	"	"	**P**	"
1812-13	"	"	**Q**	"
1813-14	"	"	**R**	"
1814-15	"	"	**S**	"
1815-16	"	"	**T**	"
1816-17	"	"	**U**	"

CYCLE VI

	CASTLE	LION PASSANT	DATE LETTER	DUTY MARK
1817-18	🏰	🦁	**a**	👤
1818-19	"	"	**b**	"
1819-20	"	"	**c**	"
GEO.IV 1820-21	"	"	**d**	"
1821-22	"	"	**e**	"
1822-23	"	"	**f**	👤
1823-24	"	"	**g**	"
1824-25	"	"	**h**	"
1825-26	"	"	**i**	"
1826-27	"	"	**k**	"
1827-28	"	"	**l**	"
1828-29	"	"	**m**	"
1829-30	"	"	**n**	"
WM.IV 1830-31	"	"	**o**	"
1831-32	🏰	🦁	**p**	👤
1832-33	"	"	**q**	"
1833-34	🏰	🦁	**r**	"
1834-35	"	"	**s**	👤
1835-36	"	"	**t**	"
1836-37	"	"	**u**	"

* This date letter also appears with a canted square punch.

† The date letter appears with alternative punch shape. **B**

CYCLE VII

	CASTLE	LION PASSANT	DATE LETTER	DUTY MARK
VICT. 1837-38	🏰	🦁	𝕬	𝐎
1838-39	"	"	𝕭	𝐎
1839-40	"	"	𝕮	𝐎
1840-41	"	"	𝕯	"
1841-42	🏰	"	𝕰	"
1842-43	"	"	𝕱	"
1843-44	🏰	"	𝕲	"
1844-45	"	"	𝕳	"
1845-46	"	"	𝕵	"
1846-47	"	"	𝕶	"
1847-48	"	"	𝕷	"
1848-49	"	"	𝕸	"
1849-50	"	"	𝕹	"
1850-51	"	"	𝕺	"
1851-52	"	"	𝕻	"
1852-53	"	"	𝕼	"
1853-54	"	"	𝕽	"
1854-55	"	"	𝕾	"
1855-56	"	"	𝕿	"
1856-57	"	"	𝖀	"

CYCLE VIII

	CASTLE	LION PASSANT	DATE LETTER	DUTY MARK
1857-58*	🏰	🦁	𝐀	🙂
1858-59	"	"	𝐁	"
1859-60	"	"	𝐂	"
1860-61	"	"	𝐃	"
1861-62	"	"	𝐄	"
1862-63	"	"	𝐅	"
1863-64	"	"	𝐆	"
1864-65	"	"	𝐇	"
1865-66	"	"	𝐈	"
1866-67	"	"	𝐊	"
1867-68	"	"	𝐋	"
1868-69	"	"	𝐌	"
1869-70	"	"	𝐍	"
1870-71	"	"	𝐎	"
1871-72	"	"	𝐏	"
1872-73	"	"	𝐐	"
1873-74	"	"	𝐑	"
1874-75	"	"	𝐒	"
1875-76	"	"	𝐓	"
1876-77	"	"	𝐔	"

* Variation of date letter

CYCLE IX

	CASTLE	LION PASSANT	DATE LETTER	DUTY MARK
1877-78	🏰	🦁	**A**	👤
1878-79	"	"	**B**	"
1879-80	"	"	**C**	"
1880-81	"	"	**D**	"
1881-82	"	"	**E**	"
1882-83	"	"	**F**	"

Assay Office closed 1883.

MARK	MAKER	PERIOD	COMMENTS
	John Elston	Early 18th C	Fine work, wide range
GF	George Ferris	1st ½ 19th C	Mostly flatware
GT	George Turner	Early 19th C	Mostly flatware
	John Elston, jun	1st ½ 18th C	Fine work, wide range
	Thomas Eustace	Late 18th C	Mostly flatware
JH	Joseph Hicks	Late 18th/Early 19th C	Mostly flatware
JO / I·O	John Osment " "	1st ½ 19th C " "	Flatware
I·S / I·S	John Stone " "	Mid 19th C " "	Mostly flatware
JW	James Williams	Mid 19th C	Flatware
JW &Cº / JW & JW	Josiah Williams & Co James & Josiah Williams	Mid 19th C " "	The firm of Williams made vast quantities of flatware in Bristol
PS	Pentecost Symonds (of Plymouth) — sterling mark	1st ½ 18th C	Fine work, wide range
RF	Richard Ferris	Late 18th/Early 19th C	Mostly flatware
RW IW JW	Robert, James & Josiah Williams	Mid 19th C	The firm of Williams made vast quantities of flatware in Bristol
SB	Samuel Blachford (Plymouth)	1st ½ 18th C	Good work, wide range
SOBEY	W R Sobey	Mid 19th C	Flatware
Sp	Pentecost Symonds (of Plymouth) see PS for his sterling mark	1st ½ 18th C	Fine work, wide range
TB	Thomas Blake	Mid 18th C	Mostly flatware
TE	Thomas Eustace	Late 18th C	Mostly flatware
WRS	William Rawlings Sobey	Mid 19th C	Flatware
W W / WW	William Woodman (Bristol)	1st ½ 19th C " "	Mostly flatware

CHAPTER VII

Glasgow

Cycles of Hallmarks

CYCLE I

	TREE FISH & BELL	DATE LETTER
1681-82	[mark]	a
1682-83		b
1683-84	[mark]	c
1684-85		d
1685-86	″	e
1686-87		f
1687-88		g
1688-89		h
1689-90	[mark]	ii
1690-91	″	k
1691-92		l
1692-93		m
1693-94		n
1694-95	[mark]	o
1695-96		p
1696-97	″	q
1697-98		r
1698-99	[mark]	s
1699-1700	[mark]	t
1700-1	[mark]	u
1701-2	″	v
1702-3		w
1703-4		x
1704-5	″	y
1705-6	″	z

'CYCLE' II

	TREE FISH & BELL	DATE LETTER
1706-7		A
1707-8	[mark]	B
1709-10	″	D
1709-10	[mark]	″
1709-20	[mark]	
1717-49	″	
1728-31	″	S
1725-35	″	S
1743-52	[mark]	S
1747-60		S
1756-76	″	S
1756-76	″	S
1757-80	[mark]	
1757-80	[mark]	″
1757-80	[mark]	O
1761-65	″	S
1763-84	[mark]	
1763-84	″	E
1763-84	″	F
1776-84	[mark]	
1777-84	[mark]	S
1781-84	[mark]	S
1782-84	[mark]	
1783-84	[mark]	″
1784-85	[mark]	S
1784-85	″	O

CYCLE III

	TREE FISH & BELL	LION RAMPANT	DATE LETTER	DUTY MARK
1819-20	🜨	🦁	**A**	👤
GEO.IV 1820-21	🜨	"	**B**	"
1821-22	"	"	**C**	"
1822-23	"	"	**D**	"
1823-24	"	"	**E**	"
1824-25	"	"	**F**	"
1825-26	"	"	**G**	"
1826-27	"	"	**H**	"
1827-28	"	"	**I**	"
1828-29	"	"	**J**	"
1829-30	"	"	**K**	"
WM.IV 1830-31	"	"	**L**	"
1831-32	"	"	**M**	"
1832-33	"	"	**N**	👤
1833-34	"	"	**O**	"
1834-35	"	"	**P**	"
1835-36	"	"	**Q**	"
1836-37	"	"	**R**	"
VICT. 1837-38	"	"	**S**	"
1838-39	"	"	**T**	"
1839-40	"	"	**U**	"
1840-41	"	"	**V**	"
1841-42	"	"	**W**	👤
1842-43	"	"	**X**	"
1843-44	"	"	**Y**	"
1844-45	"	"	**Z**	"

CYCLE IV

	TREE FISH & BELL	LION RAMPANT	DATE LETTER	DUTY MARK
1845-46	🜨	🦁	**A**	👤
1846-47	"	"	**B**	"
1847-48	"	"	**C**	"
1848-49	"	"	**D**	"
1849-50	"	"	**E**	"
1850-51	"	"	**f**	"
1851-52	"	"	**G**	"
1852-53	"	"	**H**	"
1853-54	"	"	**I**	"
1854-55	"	"	**J**	"
1855-56	"	"	**K**	"
1856-57	"	"	**L**	"
1857-58	"	"	**M**	"
1858-59	"	"	**N**	"
1859-60	"	"	**O**	"
1860-61	"	"	**P**	"
1861-62	"	"	**Q**	"
1862-63	"	"	**R**	"
1863-64	"	"	**S**	"
1864-65	"	"	**T**	"
1865-66	"	"	**U**	"
1866-67	"	"	**V**	"
1867-68*	"	"	**W**	"
1868-69	"	"	**X**	"
1869-70	"	"	**Y**	"
1870-71	"	"	**Z**	"

* 🅕 struck in addition to the above on imported wares from 1867-1904.

CYCLE V

	TREE FISH & BELL	LION RAMPANT	DATE LETTER	DUTY MARK
1871-72	🛡	🦁	**A**	☺
1872-73	"	"	**B**	"
1873-74	"	"	**C**	"
1874-75	"	"	**D**	"
1875-76	"	"	**E**	"
1876-77	"	"	**F**	"
1877-78	"	"	**G**	"
1878-79	"	"	**H**	"
1879-80	"	"	**I**	"
1880-81	"	"	**J**	"
1881-82	"	"	**K**	"
1882-83	"	"	**L**	"
1883-84	"	"	**M**	"
1884-85	"	"	**N**	"
1885-86	"	"	**O**	"
1886-87	"	"	**P**	"
1887-88	"	"	**Q**	"
1888-89	"	"	**R**	"
1889-90	"	"	**S**	"
1890-91	"	"	**T**	
1891-92	"	"	**U**	
1892-93	"	"	**V**	
1893-94	"	"	**W**	
1894-95	"	"	**X**	
1895-86	"	"	**Y**	
1896-97	"	"	**Z**	

CYCLE VI

	TREE FISH & BELL	LION RAMPANT	THISTLE	DATE LETTER
1897-98	🛡	🦁		*A*
1898-99	"	"		*B*
1899-1900	"	"		*C*
1900-1	"	"		*D*
EDW.VII 1901-2	"	"		*E*
1902-3	"	"		*F*
1903-4*	"	"		*G*
1904-5	"	"		*H*
1905-6	"	"		*I*
1906-7	"	"		*J*
1907-8	"	"		*K*
1908-9	"	"		*L*
1909-10	"	"		*M*
1910-11	"	"		*N*
1911-12	"	"		*O*
1912-13	"	"		*P*
1913-14	"	"		*Q*
1914-15	"	"	🌼	*R*
1915-16	"	"	"	*S*
1916-17	"	"	"	*T*
1917-18	"	"	"	*U*
1918-19	"	"	"	*V*
1919-20	"	"	"	*W*
1920-21	"	"	"	*X*
1921-22	"	"	"	*Y*
1922-23	"	"	"	*Z*

* **F** struck in addition to the above on imported wares from 1867-1904.

CYCLE VII

	TREE FISH & BELL	LION RAMPANT	THISTLE	DATE LETTER
1923-24	🛡	🦁	🌸	**a**
1924-25	"	"	"	**b**
1925-26	"	"	"	**c**
1926-27	"	"	"	**d**
1927-28	"	"	"	**e**
1928-29	"	"	"	**f**
1929-30	"	"	"	**g**
1930-31	"	"	"	**h**
1931-32	"	"	"	**i**
1932-33	"	"	"	**j**
1933-34	"	"	"	**k**
1934-35	"	"	"	**l**
1935-36	"	"	"	**m**
1936-37	"	"	"	**n**
1937-38	"	"	"	**O**
1938-39	"	"	"	**p**
1939-40	"	"	"	**q**
1940-41	"	"	"	**r**
1941-42	"	"	"	**s**
1942-43	"	"	"	**t**
1943-44	"	"	"	**u**
1944-45	"	"	"	**v**
1945-46	"	"	"	**w**
1946-47	"	"	"	**x**
1947-48	"	"	"	**y**
1948-49	"	"	"	**z**

CYCLE VIII

	TREE FISH & BELL	LION RAMPANT	THISTLE	DATE LETTER
1949-50	🛡	🦁	🌸	**A**
1950-51	"	"	"	**B**
1951-52	"	"	"	**C**
1952-53	"	"	"	**D**
1953-54	"	"	"	**e**
1954-55	"	"	"	**F**
1955-56	"	"	"	**G**
1956-57	"	"	"	**H**
1957-58	"	"	"	**I**
1958-59	"	"	"	**L**
1959-60	"	"	"	**M**
1960-61	"	"	"	**N**
1961-62	"	"	"	**O**
1962-63	"	"	"	**P**
1963-64	"	"	"	**R**

The Glasgow Assay Office closed in 1964.

GOLD MARKS

From 1819 onwards Glasgow follows the same pattern as Edinburgh with the obvious substitution of town marks.

IMPORTED WARES ASSAYED AT GLASGOW

1904-06

GOLD				SILVER			
22ct.	🛡	·916	+ Date letter & sponsor's mark	Britannia	🛡	·9584	+ Date letter & sponsor's mark
20ct.	"	·833	"	Sterling	"	·925	"
18ct.	"	·75	"				
15ct.	"	·625	"				
12ct.	"	·5	"				
9ct.	"	·375	"				

GOLD 1906-32				SILVER 1906-64			
22ct.	🅷	·916	+ Date letter & sponsor's mark	Britannia	🅷	·9584	+ Date letter & sponsor's mark
20ct.	"	·833	"	Sterling	"	·925	"
18ct.	"	·75	"				
15ct.	"	·625	"				
12ct.	"	·5	"				
9ct.	"	·375	"				

GOLD 1932-64*

22ct.	🅷	916	+ Date letter & sponsor's mark
18ct.	"	750	"
14ct.	"	585	"
9ct.	"	·375	"

* In 1932 and from then on 14ct. replaced 15ct. and 12ct.

MARK	MAKER	PERIOD	COMMENTS
AG	Adam Graham	2nd ½ 18th C	
AM	Alxr. Mitchell	2nd ¼ 19th C	
A T&S	A. Taylor & Son	2nd ½ 19th C	
DMcC	D. McCallum	2nd ½ 19th C	
GLN	James Glen	Mid 18th C	
H&L	Hamilton & Laidlaw	2nd ½ 19th C	
H&M	Hyslop & Marshall	2nd ½ 19th C	
HM	Henry Muirhead	Mid 19th C	
IG	James Glen	Mid 18th C	
IL	John Luke II	Early 18th C	
I·L	" "	" "	
IL	" "	" "	
J&Co	Johnston & Co.	2nd ½ 19th C	
J.C	Jas. Crichton	2nd ½ 19th C	
JM	John Mitchell	2nd ¼ 19th C	
JM&S	J. Muirhead & Sons	2nd ½ 19th C	
J.McA	J. McArthur	2nd ½ 19th C	
J.McD	J. McDonald	2nd ½ 19th C	
JMcG	J. McGregor	2nd ½ 19th C	
J.McI	J. McInnes	2nd ½ 19th C	
J&WM	J. & W. Mitchell	Mid 19th C	
M&A	Muirhead & Arthur	2nd ½ 19th C	
M&C	Milne & Campbell	Mid 18th C	
M&R	Mitchell & Russell	1st ¼ 19th C	
M&S	Mitchell & Son	2nd ¼ 19th C	
M&T	Miller & Thompson	2nd ½ 19th C	

MARK	MAKER	PERIOD	COMMENTS
M.BROS	Mitchell Bros.	2nd ½ 19th C	
R&G	Reed & Garrick	2nd ½ 19th C	
RG	Robert Gray	Last ¼ 18th C	
RG	" "	" "	
RG &S	Robt. Gray & Son	1st ½/Mid 19th C	
RG&S	" "	" "	
S&R	Smith & Rait	2nd ½ 19th C	
SB GG	Barclay & Goodwin	2nd ½ 19th C	
W.A&S	W. Alexander & Son	2nd ½ 19th C	
W.M	W. Mitchell	2nd ½ 19th C	
W.M&C?	W. Miller & Co.	2nd ½ 19th C	

CHAPTER VIII

$\mathcal{N}$ewcastle

Cycles of Hallmarks

DATE APPROX.	MARKS			
1650				
1655				
1664				
1675				
1686-87				
1690				
1695				

The above is a selection of Pre-Assay Office marks intended to give a general idea of the type of marking most usually found. See *Jackson's* pp.492-3 for a comprehensive list.

CYCLE I

	THREE CASTLES	BRIT-ANNIA	LION'S HEAD ERASED	DATE LETTER
ANNE 1702-3				
1703-4	"	"	"	
1704-5	"	"	"	
1705-6	"	"	"	
1706-7	"	"	"	
1707-8		"	"	
1708-9				†
1709-10				†
1710-11				†
1711-12				
1712-13*				
1713-14				
GEO.I 1714-15				
1715-16				
1716-17				
1717-18*		"	"	
1718-19*	"	"	"	
1719-20*	"	"	"	
1720-21*	"	"	"	

CYCLE II

	THREE CASTLES	LION PASSANT	LEOPARD'S HEAD CROWNED	DATE LETTER
1721-22*				
1722-23*			"	
1723-24*	"		"	
1724-25*	"	"	"	
1725-26*				
1726-27*	"	"	"	
GEO.II 1727-28*		"		
1728-29*	"		"	
1729-30*	"	"	"	
1730-31*	"	"	"	
1731-32*	"	"	"	
1732-33*	"	"	"	
1733-34*	"	"	"	
1734-35*	"	"	"	
1735-36*	"	"	"	
1736-37*	"	"	"	
1737-38*	"	"	"	
1738-39*	"	"	"	
1739-40*	"	"	"	

* Asterisks indicate date-letters recorded in the Newcastle Goldsmiths' Company minute books.

† F was probably used during these years (i.e. F from 1707-1711).

CYCLE III

	THREE CASTLES	LION PASSANT	LEOPARD'S HEAD CROWNED	DATE LETTER
1740-41*				A
1741-42*	"	"	"	B
1742-43*	"	"	"	C
1743-44*	"	"	"	D
1744-45*	"	"	"	E
1745-46*	"	"	"	F
1746-47*				G
1747-48*	"	"	"	H
1748-49	"	"	"	I
1749-50*	"	"	"	K
1750-51*	"			L
1751-52*	"	"	"	M
1752-53*	"	"	"	N
1753-54*	"	"	"	O
1754-55*	"	"	"	P
1755-56*	"	"	"	Q
1756-57*	"	"	"	R
1757-58*		"		S
1758-59				‡

* Asterisks indicate date letters recorded in the Newcastle Goldsmiths' Company minute books.

‡ S was probably used for 1758/59 (i.e. S from 1757-59)

CYCLE IV

	THREE CASTLES	LION PASSANT	LEOPARD'S HEAD CROWNED	DATE LETTER	DUTY MARK
1759-60*				A	
GEO.III 1760-61 to 1768	"	"	"	B	
1769-70*	"	"	"	C	
1770-71*		"		D	
1771-72*	"	"	"	E	
1772-73*		"	"	F	
1773-74*	"	"	"	G	
1774-75*	"	"	"	H	
1775-76*	"	"	"	I	
1776-77*	"	"	"	K	
1777-78*	"	"	"	L	
1778-79*	"	"	"	M	
1779-80*	"			N	
1780-81*	"	"	"	O	
1781-82	"	"	"	P	
1782-83	"	"	"	Q	
1783-84	"	"	"	R	
1784-85	"	"	"	S	
1785-86*	"	"	"	T	"
1786-87*	"	"	"	U	
1787-88*	"			W	"
1788-89*	"	"	"	X	"
1789-90*	"	"	"	Y	"
1790-91*	"	"	"	Z	"

CYCLE V

	LION PASSANT	THREE CASTLES	LEOPARD'S HEAD CROWNED	DUTY LETTER	DATE LETTER
1791-92*	🦁	🏰	👑	😊	**A**
1792-93*	"	"	"	"	**B**
1793-94*	"	"	"	"	**C**
1794-95*	"	"	"	"	**D**
1795-96*	"	"	"	"	**E**
1796-97*	"	"	"	"	**F**
1797-98*	"	"	"	"	**G**
1798-99	"	"	"	😊	**H**
1799-1800*	"	"	"	"	**I**
1800-1*	🦁	🏰	👑	😊	**K**
1801-2*	"	"	"	"	**L**
1802-3*	"	"	"	"	**M**
1803-4*	"	"	"	"	**N**
1804-5*	🦁	"	"	😊	**O**
1805-6*	"	"	"	"	**P**
1806-7*	"	"	"	"	**Q**
1807-8*	"	"	"	"	**R**
1808-9*	"	"	"	"	**S**
1809-10*	🦁	🏰	👑	😊	**T**
1810-11*	"	"	"	"	**U**
1811-12*	"	"	"	"	**W**
1812-13*	"	"	"	"	**X**
1813-14*	"	"	"	"	**Y**
1814-15*	"	"	"	"	**Z**

CYCLE VI

	DATE LETTER	DUTY MARK	LION PASSANT	THREE CASTLES	LEOPARD'S HEAD CROWNED
1815-16*	**A**	😊	🦁	🏰	👑
1816-17*	**B**	"	"	"	"
1817-18*	**C**	"	"	"	"
1818-19*	**D**	"	"	"	"
1819-20*	E	"	"	"	"
GEO.IV 1820-21*	**F**	"	"	"	"
1821-22*	**G**	😊	"	"	"
1822-23*	**H**	"	"	"	"
1823-24*	**I**	"	"	"	"
1824-25*	**K**	"	"	"	"
1825-26*	L	"	"	"	"
1826-27*	M	"	"		"
1827-28*	N	"	"	"	"
1828-29*	O	"	"	"	"
1829-30*	**P**	😊	🦁	🏰	"
WM.IV 1830-31*	Q	"	"	"	"
1831-32*	R	"	"	"	"
1832-33*	**S**	😊	"	"	"
1833-34*	T	"	"	"	"
1834-35*	**U**	"	"	"	"
1835-36*	W	"	"	"	"
1836-37*	X	"	"	"	"
VICT. 1837-38*	**Y**	"	"	"	"
1838-39*	**Z**	"	"	"	"

* Asterisks indicate date letters recorded in the Newcastle Goldsmiths' Company minute books.

CYCLE VII

	DUTY MARK	LION PASSANT	THREE CASTLES	LEOPARD'S HEAD CROWNED	DATE LETTER
1839* †	◑	🦁	🏰	👑	**A**
1840-41*	"	"	"	"	**B**
1841-42*	◑	"	"	"	**C**
1842-43*	"	"	"	"	**D**
1843-44*	"	"	"	"	E
1844-45*	"	"	"	"	F
1845-46*	"	"	"	"	G
1846-47* ‡	"	🦁	🏰	👑	**H**
1847-48*	"	"	"	"	I
1848-49*	"	"	"	"	J
1849-50*	"	"	"	"	K
1850-51*	"	"	"	"	L
1851-52*	👑	"	"	👑	**M**
1852-53*	"	"	"	"	N
1853-54*	"	"	"	"	**O**
1854-55*	"	"	"	"	P
1855-56*	"	"	"	"	Q
1856-57*	"	"	"	"	R
1857-58*	"	"	"	"	S
1858-59*	"	"	"	"	T
1859-60*	"	"	"	"	U
1860-61*	"	"	"	"	W
1861-62*	"	"	"	"	X
1862-63*	"	"	"	"	Y
1863-64*	"	"	"	"	Z

CYCLE VIII

	DUTY MARK	LION PASSANT	THREE CASTLES	LEOPARD'S HEAD CROWNED	DATE LETTER
1864-65*	👑	🦁	🏰	👑	**a**
1865-66*	"	"	"	"	b
1866-67*	"	"	"	"	c
1867-68*	"	"	"	"	d
1868-69*	"	"	"	"	e
1869-70*	"	"	"	"	**f**
1870-71*	"	"	"	"	g
1871-72*	"	"	"	"	h
1872-73*	"	"	"	"	i
1873-74*	"	"	"	"	k
1874-75*	"	"	"	"	l
1875-76*	"	"	"	"	m
1876-77*	"	"	"	"	n
1877-78*	"	"	"	"	o
1878-79*	"	"	"	"	p
1879-80*	"	"	"	"	q
1880-81*	"	"	"	"	r
1881-82*	"	"	"	"	**s**
1882-83*	"	"	"	"	t
1883-84*	"	"	"	"	u

The office was closed in 1884.

* Asterisks indicate date letters recorded in the Newcastle Goldsmith's Company minute books.

† Head of William IV has been noted as late as 1842-43.

‡ From 1846 both crowned and uncrowned leopard's heads have been found.

MARK	MAKER	PERIOD	COMMENTS
AC	Alexander Cameron (of Dundee)	2nd ¼ 19th C	Much flatware
A·R	Ann Robertson	Early 19th C	Wide range
Ba	Francis Batty I	Late 17th/Very Early 18th C	Fine maker, wide range of pieces
Ba	Francis Batty II	Early 18th C	Wide variety
CAM ERON	Alexander Cameron (of Dundee)	2nd ¼ 19th C	Much flatware
CJR	Reid & Sons	Mid 19th C	Mostly retailing by this date
CJR	" "	" "	
CR	Christian Ker Reid I	Very late 18th/Early 19th C	
CR DR	Reid & Son	Early 19th C	The last large silversmiths in Newcastle
CR DR	" "	2nd ¼ 19th C	
CR DR CR	Reid & Sons	" "	
DC	David Crawford	3rd ¼ 18th C	Wide range; much flatware
D·D	David Darling	Very late 18th/Early 19th C	Mostly small pieces
D·L	Dorothy Langlands	Early 19th C	Prolific maker
DR	Reid & Sons	Mid 19th C	Mostly retailing by this date
DR	" "	" "	
FB	Francis Batty II	Early 18th C	Wide variety
I·C	Isaac Cookson	2nd ¼ 18th C	Prolific maker
JC	" "	" "	
JC	" "	Mid 18th C	
IC	James Crawford	2nd ½ 18th C	Wide range

MARK	MAKER	PERIOD	COMMENTS
I·K	James Kirkup	1st ½ 18th C	Wide variety, good maker
I·L	John Langlands II	Very late 18th C	Prolific maker
I·L I·R	John Langlands I & John Robertson I	Last ¼ 18th C	Prolific makers, many tankards and mugs
I·L I·R	" "	" "	
I·L	John Langlands I	2nd ½ 18th C	
IR	James Kirkup	1st ½ 18th C	Wide variety, good maker
I·R	John Robertson I	Very late 18th C	Wide range
IR	John Robertson II	Early 19th C	Wide range
J·L	John Langlands I	2nd ½ 18th C	Prolific maker, many tankards and mugs
JR	John Robertson I	Very late 18th C	Wide range
Kj	James Kirkup	1st ½ 18th C	Wide variety, good maker
Ma Ba	Robert Makepeace I & Francis Batty II	Early 18th C	
R·M	Robert Makepeace I	2nd ¼ 18th C	Fine maker
R·M	" "	Mid 18th C	
T·W	Thomas Watson	Late 18th C	Prolific maker, wide range
JW	" "	Early 19th C mark	
W·B	William Beilby	Mid 18th C	Father of the famous Ralph Beilby

CHAPTER IX
Norwich

Cycles of Hallmarks

	CASTLE OVER LION	DATE LETTER
1565-66		**A**
1566-67	"	**B**
1567-68		**C**
1568-69		**D**
1569-70		**E**
1570-71		**F**

DATE (ABOUT)	CASTLE OVER LION
c.1572	
c.1580	
1590	
1600-10	

	CASTLE OVER LION	ROSE CROWNED	DATE LETTER
1624-25			**A**
1625-26	"	"	**B**
1626-27		"	**C**
1627-28	"	"	**D**
1628-29		"	**E**
1629-30			**F**
1630-31	"		**G**
1631-32	"	"	**H**
1632-33	"	"	**I**
1633-34	"	"	**K**
1634-35	"	"	**L**
1635-36			**M**
1636-37			**N**
1637-38			**O**
1638-39	"	"	**P**
1639-40			**Q**
1640-41	"	"	**R**
1641-42	"	"	**S**
1642-43	"	"	**T**

DATE (ABOUT)	MARKS
1645	
1650	

DATE (ABOUT)	MARKS
1661	
1665	
1670	
1675	
1676	
1679	
1680	
1685	
c.1685	

	ROSE CROWNED	CASTLE OVER LION	DATE LETTER
1688			a
1689			b
1690			c
1691			d
1692			E
1693			F
1694			G
1695			H
1696	"	"	I
			"
1697*	"	"	K

* Up to 27 March, 1697.

DATE (ABOUT)	MARKS
c.1697/1701	
	"
	'EH' "

DATE (ABOUT)	MARKS
1702/3	

The makers given below produced a variety of pieces, however, spoons will mostly be found.

MARK	MAKER	PERIOD	COMMENTS
	Arthur Haselwood	Mid 17th C	
	" "	" "	
	Arthur Haselwood II	3rd ¼ 17th C	
	Elizabeth Haselwood	Late 17th C	
	" "	" "	
	James Daniel	Late 17th C	
	" "	" "	
	Thomas Havers	Last ¼ 17th C	
	Timothy Skottowe	2nd ¼ 17th C	
	" "	" "	

CHAPTER X
Sheffield
Cycles of Hallmarks

CYCLE I

STANDARD MARKS

	LION PASSANT	CROWN	DATE LETTER	DUTY MARK
1773-74	🦁	👑	C	
1774-75	"	"	F	
1775-76	"	"	P	
1776-77	"	"	R	
1777-78	"	"	H	
1778-79	"	"	S	
1779-80	"	"	A	
1780-81	"	"	U	
1781-82	"	"	D	
1782-83	"	"	G	
1783-84	"	"	B	
Up to 30 Nov 1784	"	"	I	
From 1 Dec 1784-85	"	"	"	👤
1785-86	"	"	V	"
1786-87	"	👑	k	"
	"	"	"	👤
1787-88	"	"	C	"
1788-89	"	"	W	"
1789-90	"	"	SQ	"
1790-91	"	"	L	"
1791-92	"	"	P	"
1792-93	🦁	👑	U	"
1793-94	"	"	O	"
1794-95	"	"	m	"
1795-96	"	"	q	"
1796-97*	"	"	Z	"
1797	"	"	X	"
15 July 1797 to end of Aug 1798	"	"	"	👤👤
1798-99	"	"	V	👤

MARKS ON SMALL ARTICLES

	LION PASSANT	CROWN & DATE LETTER	DUTY MARK
1780-81	🦁	7	
1781-82	"	D	
1782-83	"	G	
1783-84	"	R	
Up to 30 Nov 1784	"	I	
From 1 Dec 1784-85	"	"	👤
1785-86	"	V	"
	"	"	👤
1786-87	"	k	"
1787-88	"	C	"
1788-89	"	W	"
1789-90	"	S	"
1790-91	"	L	"
1791-92	"	P	"
1792-93	"	U	"
1793-94	"	O	"
1794-95	"	m	"
1795-96	"	q	"
1796-97	"	Z	"
1797	"	X	"
15 July 1797 to end of Aug 1798	"	"	👤👤
1798-99	"	V	👤

* A teapot of 1796-97 is stamped with a variation of the Z **Z**

CYCLE II

STANDARD MARKS

	LION PASSANT	CROWN	DATE LETTER	DUTY MARK
1799-1800	🦁	👑	E	👤
1800-1	"	"	N	"
1801-2	"	"	H	"
1802-3	"	"	M	"
1803-4	"	"	F	"
1804-5	"	"	G	"
1805-6	"	"	B	👤
1806-7	"	"	A	👤
1807-8	"	"	S	"
1808-9	"	"	P	"
1809-10	"	"	K	"
1810-11	"	"	L	"
1811-12*	"	"	C	👤
1812-13	"	"	D	"
1813-14	"	"	R	"
1814-15	"	"	W	👤
1815-16	"	"	O	"
1816-17	"	"	T	"
1817-18	"	"	X	"
1818-19	"	"	I	"
1819-20	"	"	V	"
GEO.IV 1820-21	"	"	Q	"
1821-22	"	"	Y	"
1822-23	"	"	Z	"
1823-24	"	"	U	"

MARKS ON SMALL ARTICLES

	LION PASSANT	CROWN & DATE LETTER	DUTY MARK
1799-1800	🦁	E	👤
1800-1	"	N	"
1801-2	"	H	"
1802-3	"	M	"
1803-4	"	F	"
1804-5	"	G	"
1805-6	"	B	👤
1806-7	"	A	👤
1807-8	"	S	"
1808-9	"	P	"
1809-10	"	K	"
1810-11	"	L	"
1811-12*	"	C	👤
1812-13	"	D	"
1813-14	"	R	"
1814-15	"	W	👤
1815-16	"	O	"
1816-17	"	T	"
1817-18	"	X	"
1818-19	"	I	"
1819-20	"	V	"
GEO.IV 1820-21	"	Q	"
1821-22	"	Y	"
1822-23	"	Z	"
1823-24	"	U	"

* Alternative duty mark for this year 👤

CYCLE III

STANDARD MARKS

	LION PASSANT	CROWN	DATE LETTER	DUTY MARK
1824-25	🦁	👑	a	👤
1825-26	"	"	b	"
1826-27	"	"	c	"
1827-28	"	"	d	"
1828-29	"	"	e	"
1829-30	"	"	f	"
WM.IV 1830-31	"	"	g	"
1831-32	"	"	h	👤
1832-33	"	"	K	"
1833-34	"	"	l	"
1834-35	"	"	m	"
1835-36	"	"	p	👤
1836-37	"	"	q	"
VICT. 1837-38	"	"	r	"
1838-39	"	"	S	"
1839-40	"	"	t	"
1840-41	"	"	u	👤
1841-42	"	"	V	"
1842-43	"	"	X	"
1843-44	"	"	Z	"

MARKS ON SMALL ARTICLES

	LION PASSANT	CROWN & DATE LETTER	DUTY MARK
1824-25	🦁	a	👤
1825-26	"	b	"
1826-27	"	c	"
1827-28	"	d	"
1828-29	"	e	"
1829-30	"	f	"
WM.IV 1830-31	"	g	"
1831-32	"	h	👤
1832-33	"	k	"
1833-34	"	l	"
1834-35	"		"
1835-36*	"	p	👤
1836-37	"	q	"
VICT. 1837-38	"	r	"
1838-39	"	S	"
1839-40	"	t	"
1840-41	"	u	👤
1841-42	"	V	"
1842-43	"	X	"
1843-44	"	Z	"

* Variation: 🖼 P

CYCLE IV

STANDARD MARKS

	CROWN	DATE LETTER	LION PASSANT	DUTY MARK
1844-45	👑	**A**	🦁	😎
1845-46	"	**B**	"	"
1846-47	"	**C**	"	"
1847-48	"	**D**	"	"
1848-49	"	**E**	"	"
1849-50	"	**F**	"	"
1850-51	"	**G**	"	"
1851-52	"	**H**	"	"
1852-53	"	**I**	"	"
1853-54	"	**K**	"	"
1854-55	"	**L**	"	"
1855-56	"	**M**	"	"
1856-57	"	**N**	"	"
1857-58	"	**O**	"	"
1858-59	"	**P**	"	"
1859-60	"	**R**	"	"
1860-61	"	**S**	"	"
1861-62	"	**T**	"	"
1862-63	"	**U**	"	"
1863-64	"	**V**	"	"
1864-65	"	**W**	"	"
1865-66	"	**X**	"	"
1866-67	"	**Y**	"	"
1867-68	"	**Z**	"	"

MARKS ON SMALL ARTICLES

	CROWN & DATE LETTER	LION PASSANT	DUTY MARK
1844-45	**A👑**	🦁	😎
1845-46	**B👑**	"	"
1846-47	**C👑**	"	"
1847-48	**D👑**	"	"
1848-49	**E👑**	"	"
1849-50	**F👑**	"	"
1850-51	**G👑**	"	"
1851-52	**H👑**	"	"
1852-53	**I👑**	"	"
1853-54	**K👑**	"	"

CYCLE V

	CROWN	LION PASSANT	DATE LETTER	DUTY MARK
1868-69	👑	🦁	**A**	👤
1869-70	"	"	**B**	"
1870-71	"	"	**C**	"
1871-72	"	"	**D**	"
1872-73	"	"	**E**	"
1873-74	"	"	**F**	"
1874-75	"	"	**G**	"
1875-76	"	"	**H**	"
1876-77	"	"	**J**	"
1877-78	"	"	**K**	"
1878-79	"	"	**L**	"
1879-80	"	"	**M**	"
1880-81	"	"	**N**	"
1881-82	"	"	**O**	"
1882-83	"	"	**P**	"
1883-84	"	"	**Q**	"
1884-85	"	"	**R**	"
1885-86	"	"	**S**	"
1886-87	"	"	**T**	"
1887-88	"	"	**U**	"
1888-89	"	"	**V**	"
1889-90	"	"	**W**	"
June 1890	"	"	"	
1890-91	"	"	**X**	
1891-92	"	"	**Y**	
1892-93	"	"	**Z**	

CYCLE VI

	CROWN	LION PASSANT	DATE LETTER
1893-94	👑	🦁	**a**
1894-95	"	"	**b**
1895-96	"	"	**c**
1896-97	"	"	**d**
1897-98	"	"	**e**
1898-99	"	"	**f**
1899-1900	"	"	**g**
1900-1	"	"	**h**
EDW.VII 1901-2	"	"	**i**
1902-3	"	"	**k**
1903-4	"	"	**l**
1904-5	"	"	**m**
1905-6	"	"	**n**
1906-7	"	"	**o**
1907-8	"	"	**p**
1908-9	"	"	**q**
1909-10	"	"	**r**
GEO.V 1910-11	"	"	**s**
1911-12	"	"	**t**
1912-13	"	"	**u**
1913-14	"	"	**v**
1914-15	"	"	**w**
1915-16	"	"	**x**
1916-17	"	"	**y**
1917-18	"	"	**z**

CYCLE VII

	CROWN	LION PASSANT	DATE LETTER
1918-19			a
1919-20	"	"	b
1920-21	"	"	c
1921-22	"	"	d
1922-23	"	"	e
1923-24	"	"	f
1924-25	"	"	g
1925-26	"	"	h
1926-27	"	"	i
1927-28	"	"	k
1928-29	"	"	l
1929-30	"	"	m
1930-31	"	"	n
1931-32	"	"	o
1932-33	"	"	p
1933-34*	"	"	q
1934-35*	"	"	r
1935-36	"	"	s
EDW.VIII 1936-37	"	"	t
GEO.VI 1837-38	"	"	u
1938-39	"	"	v
1939-40	"	"	w
1940-41	"	"	x
1941-42	"	"	y
1942-43	"	"	z

CYCLE VIII

	CROWN	LION PASSANT	DATE LETTER
1943-44			A
1944-45	"	"	B
1945-46	"	"	C
1946-47	"	"	D
1947-48	"	"	E
1948-49	"	"	F
1949-50	"	"	G
1950-51	"	"	H
1951-52	"	"	I
ELIZ.II 1952-53*	"	"	K
1953-54	"	"	L
1954-55	"	"	M
1955-56	"	"	N
1956-57	"	"	O
1957-58	"	"	P
1958-59	"	"	Q
1959-60	"	"	R
1960-61	"	"	S
1961-62	"	"	T
1962-63	"	"	U
1963-64	"	"	V
1964-65	"	"	W
1965-66	"	"	X
1966-67	"	"	Y
1967-68	"	"	Z

* Optional Silver Jubilee mark:

* Optional coronation mark:

CYCLE IX

	CROWN	LION PASSANT	DATE LETTER
1968-69	👑	🦁	**𝒜**
1969-70	"	"	**ℬ**
1970-71	"	"	**𝒞**
1971-72	"	"	**𝒟**
1972-73	"	"	**ℰ**
1973-74*	"	"	**𝔉**
1974 up to 31 Dec	"	"	**𝒢**

* To commemorate the bicentenary of the Sheffield Assay Office, a copy of the date letter for 1773 was used (in a different field to avoid confusion).

CYCLE X

	ROSE	LION PASSANT	DATE LETTER
1975	🌹	🦁	**𝒜**
1976	"	"	**ℬ**
1977 †	"	"	**𝒞**
1978	"	"	**𝒟**
1979	"	"	**ℰ**
1980	"	"	**ℱ**
1981	"	"	**𝒢**
1982	"	"	**ℋ**
1983	"	"	**𝒥**
1984	"	"	**𝒦**
1985	"	"	**ℒ**
1986	"	"	**ℳ**
1987	"	"	**𝒩**
1988	"	"	**𝒪**
1989	"	"	**𝒫**
1990	"	"	**𝒬**
1991	"	"	**ℛ**

† Optional Silver Jubilee mark: 👤

Marks reproduced courtesy The Worshipful Company of Goldsmiths.

PLATINUM FROM 1975 ON

	ROSE	PLATINUM MARK	DATE LETTER
Date as Left	🌹	⬠	**𝒜**

GOLD MARKS

22ct.	✿	♔	**22**	**C**
18ct.	"	"	**18**	"
15ct.			**15** **·625**	"
12ct.			**12** **·5**	"
9ct.			**9** **375**	"

Sheffield has put hallmarks on gold since 1904. The examples given are for 1920-1. In 1932 15 and 12 carats were abolished and replaced by 14 carats (marked 14·585). From 1932 to the end of 1974 the four carat values of 22, 18, 14, and 9 will be found marked 22, 18, 14·585 and 9·375 respectively.

From 1 January, 1975 to the present day 22 carat is represented by 916, 18 carat by 750, 14 by 585 and 9 carat by 375. As with the earlier gold marks these punches will be struck with a crown, the rose for Sheffield and the date letter.

IMPORTED WARES ASSAYED AT SHEFFIELD

The letter F was added, as for example:

	CROWN	LION PASSANT	DATE LETTER	IMPORT MARK
1893-94	♔	🦁	**a**	**F**

IMPORT MARKS 1904-06

	GOLD			SILVER			
22ct.	✹	**22·916**	+ Date letter & sponsor's mark	Britannia	✹	**·9584**	+ Date letter & sponsor's mark
20ct.	"	**20·833**	"	Sterling	"	**·925**	"
18ct.	"	**18·75**	"				
15ct.	"	**15·625**	"				
12ct.	"	**12·5**	"				
9ct.	"	**9·375**	"				

	GOLD 1906-32			SILVER 1906 to end of 1974			
22ct.	**Ω**	**22·916**	+ Date letter & sponsor's mark	Britannia	**Ω**	**·9584**	+ Date letter & sponsor's mark
20ct.	"	**20·833**	"	Sterling	"	**·925**	"
18ct.	"	**18·75**	"				
15ct.	"	**15·625**	"				
12ct.	"	**12·5**	"				
9ct.	"	**9·375**	"				

IMPORT MARKS (continued)

GOLD 1932 to end of 1974

22ct.	Ω	916
18ct.	"	750
14ct.	"	585
9ct.	"	375

1975 and on

Platinum	Ω	950
Gold 22ct.	Ω	916
18ct.	"	750
14ct.	"	585
9ct.	"	375

Silver Britannia	Ω	958
Sterling	"	925

CONVENTION HALLMARKS

Precious Metal		Town Mark	Fineness Mark	Common Control Mark
Platinum		⬤	950	950
Gold	18ct.	"	750	750
	14ct.	"	585	585
	9ct.	"	375	375
Silver	Sterling	"	925	925

ON IMPORTED WARES

Precious Metal		Town Mark	Fineness Mark	Common Control Mark
Platinum		Ω	950	950
Gold	18ct.	Ω	750	750
	14ct.	"	585	585
	9ct.	"	375	375
Silver	Sterling	Ω	925	925

MARK	MAKER	PERIOD	COMMENTS
AG&Cº	Alex Goodman & Co	(First entered 1797; this mark 1801)	Large range
DH&Cº	Daniel Holy & Co	(Entered 1783)	Large range
E M&Cº	Elkington Mason & Co	(Entered 1859)	Large variety
GA &Cº	George Ashworth	(Entered 1773)	Large range
GE &Cº	George Eadon & Co	(Entered 1795)	Large range
H&H	Howard & Hawksworth	(Entered 1835)	Large variety
HE &Cº	Hawkesworth, Eyre & Co	(Entered 1833)	Large variety
HT&Cº	Hy Tudor & Co	(Entered 1797)	Large range
H·L T·L	Tudor & Leader	(Entered 1773)	Large range
HW &Co HW &Cº	Hy Wilkinson & Co	(Entered 1831)	Large variety
I&IW &Cº	Waterhouse, Hodson & Co	(Entered 1822)	Candlesticks
IG&Cº	John Green & Co	(Entered 1793)	Prolific maker of candlesticks
IH&Cº IH Cº	J Hoyland & Co " "	(Entered 1773) " "	Large range
I·K·I·W&Cº	Kirkby, Waterhouse & Co	(Entered c.1813)	Prolific maker, wide range
I·P&Cº	John Parsons & Co	(Entered 1783)	Prolific maker of candlesticks
I·R&Cº	John Roberts & Co	(Entered 1805)	Prolific maker, large range
ITY &Cº	J T Younge & Co	(Entered 1797)	Large range
ITY&Cº	John Younge & Sons	(Entered 1788)	Large range
IW&Cº	John Winter & Co	(Entered 1773)	Large range
J.D &S	James Deakin & Sons	(Entered 1894)	Large variety
J·D&S	James Dixon & Son	(Entered 1867)	Large variety

MARK	MAKER	PERIOD	COMMENTS
JD WD	James Deakin & Sons	(Entered 1878)	Large variety
JR	John Round & Son Ltd	(Entered 1874)	Large variety
M&W	Mappin & Webb	(Entered 1892)	Large variety
MB	Mappin Bros	(Entered 1859)	Large variety
MF &Co	M Fenton & Co	(Entered c.1790)	Large range
MF RC	Fenton Creswick & Co	(Entered 1773)	Large range
MH &Co	Martin Hall & Co	(Entered 1854)	Large variety
M&R&Co	Mappin & Webb	(Entered 1864)	Large variety
N·S&C?	Nathaniel Smith & Co	(Entered 1780)	Large range
R&B	Roberts & Belk	(Entered 1892)	Large variety
R·M	Richard Morton & Co	(Entered 1773 & 1781)	Large range
R·M &Co	" "	(Entered 1773)	
RM EH	Martin Hall & Co	(Entered 1863)	Large variety
RM EH	Martin Hall & Co Ltd	(Entered 1880)	
S R & C?	S Roberts & Co	(Entered 1773)	Large range
ST N&H	Smith, Tate & Co (Nicholson & Hoult)	(Entered 1812)	Prolific maker, wide range
TB &S	Thomas Bradbury & Sons	(Entered 1892)	Large variety
TJ NC	T J & N Creswick	(Entered c.1827)	Candlesticks
TJ&NC	" "	(Entered 1819)	Prolific maker, wide range
T·LAW	Thomas Law	(Entered 1773)	Large range
TW&C?	Thomas Watson & Co	(Entered c.1801)	Prolific maker, wide range
W&H	Walker & Hall	(Entered 1862)	Large variety
W&H	" "	(Entered 1896)	
WS GS	W & G Sissons	(Entered 1858)	Large variety

CHAPTER XI

York

Cycles of Hallmarks

Example of pre-1559 Town Mark

DATE	MARK
c.1475-1500	(mark)

CYCLE I

	TOWN MARK	DATE LETTER
ELIZ.I 1559-60		A
1560-61	(mark)	B
1561-62	"	C
1562-63	(mark)	D
1563-64		E
1564-65	(mark)	F
1565-66		G
1566-67	(mark)	H
1567-68		I
1568-69	(mark)	K
1569-70	(mark)	L
1570-71		M
1571-72		N
1572-73	(mark)	O
1573-74		P
1574-75	"	Q
1575-76	(mark)	R
1576-77		S
1577-78	"	T
1578-79		V
1579-80		W
1580-81		X
1581-82		Y
1582-83	"	Z

CYCLE II

	TOWN MARK	DATE LETTER
1583-84	(mark)	a
1584-85	(mark)	b
1585-86		c
1586-87		d
1587-88	"	e
1588-89		f
1589-90		g
1590-91	"	h
1591-92		i
1592-93	(mark)	k
1593-94	"	l
1594-95	"	m
1595-96		n
1596-97		o
1597-98	"	p
1598-99		q
1599-1600	"	r
1600-1		s
1601-2	"	t
1602-3		u
JAS.I 1603-4		w
1604-5	"	x
1605-6		y
1606-7		z

CYCLE III

	TOWN MARK	DATE LETTER
1607-8	(mark)	A
1608-9	(mark)	B
1609-10	"	C
1610-11	"	D
1611-12	"	E
1612-13	"	F
1613-14	(mark)	G
1614-15	"	H
1615-16	(mark)	I
1616-17	"	K
1617-18		L
1618-19	"	M
1619-20	"	N
1620-21	"	O
1621-22	"	P
1622-23	(mark)	Q
1623-24	(mark)	R
1624-25	(mark)	S
CHAS.I 1625-26	(mark)	T
1626-27	"	U
1627-28	"	W
1628-29		X
1629-30	"	Y
1630-31	"	Z

CYCLE IV

	TOWN MARK	DATE LETTER
1631-32	🛡	𝑎
1632-33	🛡	𝖇
1633-34	"	𝐜
1634-35	"	𝖉
1635-36	"	𝖊
1636-37	🛡	𝖋
1637-38	🛡	𝖌
1638-39	"	𝖍
1639-40	"	𝖎
1640-41	"	𝖐
1641-42	"	𝖑
1642-43	"	𝖒
1643-44		𝑛
1644-45	"	𝖔
1645-46		𝑝
1646-47		𝑞
1647-48		𝑟
1648-49	🛡	𝖘
COMWTH. 1649-50	🛡	𝖙
1650-51	"	𝖚
1651-52		𝑤
1652-53	"	𝖝
1653-54	"	𝖞
1654-55	"	𝖟

CYCLE V

	TOWN MARK	DATE LETTER
1655-56	🛡	𝓐
1656-57	🛡	𝓑
1757-58	🛡	𝓒
1658-59	"	𝓓
1659-60	"	𝓔
CHAS.II 1660-61	🛡	𝓙
1661-62	🛡	𝓖
1662-63	"	𝓗
1663-64	"	𝓙
1664-65	🛡	𝓚
1665-66	"	𝓛
1666-67	"	𝓜
1667-68	"	𝓝
1668-69	🛡	𝓞
1669-70	"	𝓟
1670-71	🛡	𝓠
1671-72	"	𝓡
1672-73	"	𝓢
1673-74	"	𝓣
1674-75	"	𝓥
1675-76	"	𝓦
1676-77	🛡	𝓧
1677-78	"	𝓨
1678-79	"	𝓩

CYCLE VI

	TOWN MARK	DATE LETTER
1679-80	🛡	𝕬
1680-81	"	𝕭
1681-82	🛡	𝕮
1682-83		𝕯
1683-84	"	𝕰
1684-85	"	𝕱
JAS.II 1685-86	"	𝕲
1686-87	"	𝕳
1687-88		𝕵
1688-89	🛡	𝕶
WM.& MY. 1689-90	"	𝕷
1690-91	"	𝕸
1691-92		𝕹
1692-93	🛡	𝕺
1693-94	"	𝕻
1694-95	"	𝕼
1695-96	"	𝕽
WM.III 1696-97		𝕾

CYCLE VII

	TOWN MARK	BRIT-ANNIA	LION'S HEAD ERASED	DATE LETTER
1701-2	✠	🛡	🦁	𝓡
ANNE 1702-3	✠	🛡	🦁	**B**
1703-4	"	"	"	**C**
1704-5	"	"	"	**D**
1705-6				
1706-7	"	"	"	**F**
1707-8	"	"	"	**G**
1708-9				
1709-10	"	"	"	**I**
1710-11				
1711-12				
1712-13	"	"	"	**m**
1713-14				
GEO.I 1714-15	"	"	"	**O**
1715-16				

CYCLE VIII

	TOWN MARK	LION PASSANT	LEOPARD'S HEAD CROWNED	DATE LETTER	DUTY MARK
1776-77				A	
1777-78				B	
1778-79				C	
1779-80	🛡	🦁	🐆	**D**	
1780-81	"	"	"	**E**	
1781-82	"	"	"	**F**	
1782-83	"	"	"	**G**	
1783-84		"	"	**H**	
1784-85	"	"	"	**J**	👤
1785-86		"	🐆		"
1786-87		"	🐆	"	👤

*CYCLE IX

	TOWN MARK	LION PASSANT	LEOPARD'S HEAD CROWNED	DUTY MARK	DATE LETTER
1787-88		🦁	👑	🐴	**A**
1788-89					**B**
1789-90	▦	"	▦	"	**C**
1790-91	⊕	"	"	"	**d**
1791-92		"	"	"	**e**
1792-93					"
1793-94		"	"	"	**g**
1794-95		"	"	"	**h**
1795-96	"	"	"	"	**i**
1796-97		"	"	"	**k**
1797-98	"	"	"	🐴	**l**
1798-99	✚	"	"	"	**M**
1799-1800		"	"	"	**N**
1800-1	⊕	"	"	"	**O**
1801-2		"	"	"	**P**
1802-3	"	"	"	"	**Q**
1803-4	"	"	"	"	**R**
1804-5		"	"	"	**S**
1805-6		"	"	"	**T**
1806-7		"	"	"	**U**
1807-8	"	"	"	"	**V**
1808-9		"	"	"	**W**
1809-10		"	"	"	**X**
1810-11		"	"	"	**Y**
1811-12		"	"	"	**Z**

* From 1793-1808 the lion passant is sometimes found facing right.

Other variations stamped on small brass plate from the assay office:

1805-6   1807-8   1809-10

Sometimes used from 1790 onwards.

CYCLE X

	TOWN MARK	LION PASSANT	LEOPARD'S HEAD CROWNED	DUTY MARK	DATE LETTER
1812-13*		🦁	👑	👑	**a**
1813-14*					"
1814-15					"
1815-16*		"	"	"	**d**
1816-17					"
1817-18	⊕	"	"	"	**f**
1818-19	"	"	"	"	**g**
1819-20*		"	"	"	**h**
GEO.IV 1820-21*		"	"	"	**i**
1821-22*		"	"	"	**k**
1822-23		"	"		"
1823-24*					"
1824-25	"	"	"	"	**n**
1825-26	"	"	"	"	**o**
1826-27		"	"	"	**p**
1827-28§		"	"	"	**q**
1828-29		"	"	"	**r**
1829-30	"	"	"	"	**s**
WM.IV 1830-31		"	"	👑	**t**
1831-32		"	"	"	**u**
1832-33*		"	"	👑	**v**
1833-34*		"	"	"	**w**
1834-35		"	"	"	**x**
1835-36		"	"	"	**z**

* In examples of marks from 1812 onwards, the leopard's head is sometimes found with whiskers and sometimes without. Other variations stamped on small brass plate from the assay office:

1812-15 **a**   1813-14 **b**   1815-17 **d**

1819-20 **h**   1820-21 **i**   1821-24 **k**

1832-33 **u**   1833-34 **w**

§ Alternative date letter for 1827-8: (See 'Any Old Ladle', *Antique Collecting*, Dec. 1987.) **q**

CYCLE XI

	TOWN MARK	LION PASSANT	LEOPARD'S HEAD CROWNED	DUTY MARK	DATE LETTER
1836-37	🏛	🦁	👑	◯	**A**
1837-38		"	"	◯	**B**
1838-39	✚	"	"	"	**C**
1839-40	🏛	"	"	◯	**D**
1840-41		"	"	"	**E**
1841-42	"	"	"	"	**F**
1842-43		"	"	"	**G**
1843-44		"	"	"	**H**
1844-45		"	"	"	**I**
1845-46					**K**
1846-47		"	"	"	**L**
1847-48		"		"	**M**
1848-49	"	"		"	**N**
1849-50		"	"	"	**O**
1850-51		"	"	"	**P**
1851-52		"	"	"	**Q**
1852-53		"		"	**R**
1853-54		"	"	"	**S**
1854-55		"	"	"	**T**
1855-56		"	"	"	**U**
1856-57	"	"	"	"	**V**
1857-58		"	"	"	**W**
1858-59		"		"	**X**

It is thought that the York Assay Office ended its active life by the end of 1858.

MARK	MAKER	PERIOD	COMMENTS
H&P	John Hampston & John Prince	Last ¼ 18th C	Variety of plate
HP &C'	Hampston, Prince & Cattles	Very early 19th C	Variety of plate, mostly flatware
HH I·P	John Hampston & John Prince	Last ¼ 18th C	Variety of plate
I&H P	" "	" "	
I&H P	" "	" "	
JB	James Barber	Mid 19th C	Mostly flatware
JB GC W.N	James Barber, George Cattle & William North	2nd ¼ 19th C	Mostly flatware
JB WN	James Barber & William North	2nd ¼ 19th C	Mostly flatware
J B WW	James Barber & William Whitwell	Early 19th C	Variety of plate, mostly flatware
LA	John Langwith	Queen Anne period	Variety of plate
RC JB	Robert Cattle & James Barber	Early 19th C	Variety of plate, mostly flatware

NOTE: There are several variations of the above. Reference to either *Jackson's* York section or Martin Gubbins' *York Silversmiths* is recommended.

English Provincial Marks

The marks given below are intended as a selective guide to the sort of marks to be found in these centres. For a comprehensive list with names of makers and other marks, reference should be made to the appropriate section in the main volume.

Barnstaple

DATE	MARKS
c.1585	
1630-40	
1670-80	

Bridgwater

DATE	MARKS
c.1680	

Bristol

DATE	MARKS
c.1620	
c.1735	

Coventry

DATE	MARKS
Early 17th C	

Dorchester

DATE	MARKS
c.1575	

Falmouth

DATE	MARKS
c.1685-1700	

Gloucester

DATE	MARKS
c.1660-90	

Gt. Yarmouth

DATE	MARKS
c.1680	

Hull

DATE	MARKS
1629	
1651	
1697	

King's Lynn

DATE	MARKS
c.1600-20	

Launceston

DATE	MARKS
c.1695	

Leeds

DATE	MARKS
1650	
1690	

Leicester

DATE	MARKS
1570	

Lewes

DATE	MARKS
c.1640	

Lincoln

DATE	MARKS
c.1570	

Liverpool

DATE	MARKS
Early 18th C	
c.1710	

Plymouth

DATE	MARKS
1600-50	
c.1695	
1697-1700	

Salisbury

DATE	MARKS
Late 16th e.17th C	
1620-40	
1640-50	
1670	

Sherborne

DATE	MARKS
Early 17th C	

Southampton

DATE	MARKS
c.1680	

Taunton

DATE	MARKS
c.1660-80	
c.1690	

Truro

DATE	MARKS
c.1610-20	

Waveney Valley

DATE	MARKS
c.1650	

Scottish Provincial Marks

The marks given below are intended as a selective guide to the sort of marks to be found in these centres. For a comprehensive list with names of makers and other marks, reference should be made to the appropriate section in the main volume.

Aberdeen

DATE (ABOUT)	MARKS
1650	
1691-97	
1718-27	
1778-1801	
1824-91	
1871	

Arbroath

DATE (ABOUT)	MARKS
1835-50	

Banff

DATE (ABOUT)	MARKS
1698	
1750	
1820-40	
1825	

Canongate

DATE (ABOUT)	MARKS
1625	
1696	
1740	
1770-75	
1775	

Cupar

DATE (ABOUT)	MARKS
Mid 19th C	

Dumfries

DATE (ABOUT)	MARKS
1794-1817	
1820	
1834-44	

Dundee

DATE (ABOUT)	MARKS
1628-36	AL ☷ AL
1667	TL ☷ TL
1734-35	GD ☷ GD E
1790-1800	EL ☷ EL m
1820-40	CAM ERON ☷ C ☷ DUN DEE
1865	RN ☷ ☷ ☷

Elgin

DATE (ABOUT)	MARKS
1708	☷ ELGIN D
1755	IH ELN ☷ A
1813	TS ELN ☷
1835	JS ELN

Forres

DATE (ABOUT)	MARKS
1817-36	☷ IPR ☷
1850-67	RH ☷ RH

Greenock

DATE (ABOUT)	MARKS
1775-80	IT ☷ IT S
1800-30	☷ ☷ ☷ C ☷

Inverness

DATE (ABOUT)	MARKS
1708	M INS M
1760	RA ☷ C INS
1830	RN INS ☷ RN
1840	TS INS ☷
1890	F&M ☷ INVS

Montrose

DATE (ABOUT)	MARKS
1671	☷ ☷ ☷
1752	T-I B ☷
1790	☷ ☷ ☷
1835	☷ ☷ PL ☷ ☷
1860	☷ ☷ ☷ S

Paisley

DATE (ABOUT)	MARKS
1790-1820	IA ☷ IA ☷ ☷ I&GH WH ☷ ☷

Perth

DATE (ABOUT)	MARKS
1687	RG ☷ RG
1772-85	IC ☷ IC ☷
1839-56	RK ☷ RK ☷

Peterhead

DATE (ABOUT)	MARKS
1825	**WF** **PHD** **WF**

St. Andrews

DATE (ABOUT)	MARKS
1670	**PG** ⊗ **PG**

Tain

DATE (ABOUT)	MARKS
1740	**H·R** **TAIN** **S·D** ⊞
1835	**RW** **TAIN** ⊞

Wick

DATE (ABOUT)	MARKS
1825	**JS** **WICK**

Irish Provincial Marks

The marks given below are intended as a selective guide to the sort of marks to be found in these centres. For a comprehensive list with names of makers and other marks, reference should be made to the appropriate section in the main volume.

Cork

DATE	MARKS
1663	
1679	
1686	
1692	
1698	
1710	
1715-25	
1745-70	
1795	
1808-20	

Limerick

DATE	MARKS
1685	
1710	
1730-62	
1784	
1784	
1798	
1810-20	

Galway

DATE	MARKS
1695	
1730	

Kinsale

DATE	MARKS
1712	

Youghal

DATE	MARKS
1644	
1683	
1712	

Bibliography

Other than *Jackson's Silver & Gold Marks of England, Scotland & Ireland,* the following works will be found to be particularly useful.

General

Report of Departmental Committee on Hallmarking Board of Trade, 1959.

Touching Gold and Silver, Exhibition Catalogue, Goldsmiths Hall, 1978.

Castro, J.P. de, *The Law and Practice of Marking Gold and Silver Wares,* 1926.

D.T.W., *Hallmarks on Gold and Silver Plate,* J.M. Dent and Sons Ltd., 1925.

Dove, A.B.L., "Some New Light on Plate Duty and its Marks", *Antique Collecting,* Sept. 1984.

Dove, A.B.L., "Some Observations on Gold and its Hallmarks", *Antique Collecting,* Sept. 1986.

How, G.E.P. and J.P., *English and Scottish Silver Spoons and Pre-Elizabethan Hallmarks on English Plate,* 3 vols., privately printed, 1952.

How, G.E.P., *The Ellis Collection of Provincial Spoons,* Sotheby and Co. Catalogue, 1935.

London

Culme, J., *The Directory of Gold and Silversmiths, Jewellers and Allied Traders 1838-1914,* Antique Collectors' Club, 1987.

Goldsmiths' Hall — see General section.

Grimwade, A.G., *London Goldsmiths 1697-1837, Their Marks and Lives,* Faber and Faber, 3rd edition 1990.

How, G.E.P. and J.P. — see General section.

Kent, T.A., *London Silver Spoonmakers 1500-1697,* The Silver Society, 1981.

Birmingham

Jones, K.C., (ed.), *The Silversmiths of Birmingham and their Marks 1750-1980,* N.A.G. Press, 1981.

Chester

Ridgway, M.H., *Chester Goldsmiths from early times to 1726,* Sherratt, 1968.

Ridgway, M.H., *Chester Silver 1727-1837,* Phillimore, 1985.

Cornwall

Douch, H.L., "Cornish Goldsmiths", *Journal of the Royal Institution of Cornwall,* 1970.

Exeter

Exeter Museum, *Exeter and West Country Silver,* 1978.

Kent, T.A., *Early West Country Spoons,* Exeter Museum, 1977.

Ireland

Bennett, D., *Irish Georgian Silver,* Cassell and Co. Ltd., 1972.

Ticher, K., and Delamer, I., *Hallmarks on Dublin Silver 1730-1772,* National Museum of Ireland, 1968.

King's Lynn

Lynn Silver, Exhibition Catalogue, King's Lynn Preservation Trust.

Liverpool

Grosvenor Museum, The, *Chester Silver,* Loan Exhibition Catalogue, Sotheby's, 1984.

Newcastle

Gill, M.A.V., *A Directory of Newcastle Goldsmiths,* Goldsmiths Hall, 1980.

Gill, M.A.V., *A Handbook of Newcastle Silver,* 1978.

Norwich

Barrett, G.N., *Norwich Silver and its Marks, 1565-1702.*

Barrett, G.N., *The Goldsmiths of Norwich 1141-1750,* The Wensum Press, 1981.

Norfolk Museums Service, *Norwich Silver in the Collection of Norwich Castle Museum,* 1981.

Sheffield

Bradbury, F., *History of Old Sheffield Plate,* Northend Publications, 1968.

Sheffield Assay Office, *The Sheffield Assay Office Register,* 1911.

York

Gubbins, M., *York Assay Office and Silversmiths 1776-1858,* William Sessions Ltd., 1983.

Lee, W., *York Silver 1475-1858,* Catalogue of the William Lee Collection in the York Undercroft, 1972.

JACKSON'S SILVER AND GOLD MARKS OF ENGLAND, SCOTLAND AND IRELAND
edited by Ian Pickford
766 pp., ISBN 0 907462 63 4
For over 80 years this has been the book on antique silver essential to dealers, scholars and collectors. Now half a century of research is incorporated in this **new edition** which contains some 10,000 corrections to the original material as well as much vital extra information. A key reference book.

19TH CENTURY AUSTRALIAN SILVER
by J.B. Hawkins
2 volumes. Vol I, 344 pp. Vol. II, 376 pp. Over 80 colour plates. Over 700 b. & w. illustrations. ISBN 1 85149 002 7
The first comprehensive book on the fascinating but hitherto neglected wares of 19th century Australian silversmiths. It contains detailed biographies of all known Australian craftsmen with a photographic index of their marks, lavishly illustrated throughout. While a strong European design influence predominates, Australian flora and fauna play an important part in the manufacture of the more exotic pieces. An essential reference as without it, a good deal of Australian silver, usually many times more valuable than its European equivalent, will go unrecognised or wrongly ascribed. This will be the standard work for many years.

STARTING TO COLLECT SILVER
by John Luddington
228 pp., 345 b. & w. illus. ISBN 0 907462 48 0
John Luddington, an experienced dealer of long standing, describes the importance of the many varied aspects of quality both in terms of aesthetics and hard cash, and analyses the value of pieces.

This fascinating book describes in an easy to read manner the many problems and pitfalls which face the novice and includes copious illustrations of interesting items. It guides the reader through the pitfalls of the silver trade and discusses the pieces to avoid.

THE PRICE GUIDE TO ANTIQUE SILVER
2nd edition with 1992 prices
by Peter Waldron
368 pp., 1,172 b. & w. illus. ISBN 1 85149 165 1
One of our most popular titles. The head of Sotheby's silver department has used the huge number of photographs at his disposal to advise collectors on what to buy and what to avoid. Detailed examination of fakes is an important feature of this classic work.

For details of these and other books on jewellery, antique furniture, horology, architecture and gardening contact:

Antique Collectors' Club

5 Church Street
Woodbridge, Suffolk IP12 1DS, UK
Tel: 0394 385501 Fax: 0394 384434

Market Street Industrial Park
Wappingers' Falls, NY 12590, USA
Tel: 914 297 0003 Fax: 914 297 0068